# Regenerate
*Your*
# Reality

# Regenerate
## *Your*
# Reality

YOUR GUIDE TO
REGENERATIVE LIVING, HAPPINESS,
LOVE & SOVEREIGNTY

JEAN LOUISE PULLEN

Published by Publish Your Gift®
An imprint of Purposely Created Publishing Group, LLC

Printed in the United States of America

ISBN: 978-1-64484-528-8 (print)
ISBN: 978-1-64484-529-5 (ebook)

*A portion of the proceeds from this book will benefit the Trees, Training, Trade Program by Jungle Project in partnership with the Kiss the Ground nonprofit organization, whose combined missions are to preserve the quality of our soils and water through regenerative farming and agroforestry. We believe Regenerative Agriculture can reverse climate change, while providing a solution for malnutrition and world hunger. Learn more at https://www. regenerateyourreality.com/takeaction.*

"A seed is a forest inside out."
—Matshona Dhliwayo

"The significant problems we have cannot be solved at the same level of thinking with which we created them."
—Albert Einstein

"It's not the strongest species that survives, nor the most intelligent, but the most responsive to change."
—Charles Darwin

"If you are doing the right thing for the earth, she's giving you great company."
—Vandana Shiva

## SPECIAL CONTRIBUTORS

*Ahimsa Ongwenyi*

*Alan Cacao*

*Astaria Light*

*Brett Pullen*

*Camille Willemain*

*Ciara Lemony*

*Danielle Ashé*

*Diana Chaves*

*Eva Dalak*

*Gustavo Angulo*

*Lala Palmieri*

*Katie McCormick*

*Estonia Kersey Otieno*

*Paul Zink*

*Sarah Marie Wu*

*Toby Israel*

*Rea Farout*

# TABLE OF CONTENTS

# INTRODUCTION

## MY STORY

I wrote this book as a gift to myself, a reminder of who I am now and who I am becoming. My wish is that this book might also inspire others to regenerate *their* reality.

Today, I am living my dream in paradise on my Costa Rican "Fairy Farm" (*Finca de las Hadas*). My partner and I are growing much of our own food on our land with three rivers flowing through it. We live on both the Pacific and Caribbean coasts of Costa Rica, where the jungles host over 6 percent of the world's total biodiversity.[1] Costa Rica has welcomed me here, and I feel so fortunate. *¡Pura Vida!*

When I was a little girl, I would often find secret gardens in the forest. I swept the pine needles away from the forest floor to create a little space to sit and play, dwelling with the other forest fairies. I still carry this spirit of imagination and childlike play, cherishing the butterflies, hummingbirds, toucans, monkeys, and sloths that cross my path.

I live with my partner, Alan, with whom I have shared four years of adventures. Alan has been a driving force of our shared dream, teaching permaculture through action for the last thirteen years. We live with our dog, Pata

---

1 "Environment: Embajada De Costa Rica En Dc," Environment | Embajada de Costa Rica en DC, accessed November 2, 2021, http://www.costarica-embassy.org/index.php?q=node%2F12.

Blanca (White Paw), and our eleven hens. Together, Alan and I have planted thousands of edible fruit trees, along with annuals, medicinals, and perennial gardens. We produce much of what we consume and strive to walk each step with love and care for ourselves and the earth.

My favorite aspects of the day revolve around the sun. I cherish the early morning, when the birds and animals are most active and the rays of light shine through the forest canopy. I love watching sunsets as the sky turns to dusk and the insect orchestra sings.

When I look back into my history, it feels so full of lifetimes and experiences. I grew up in the suburbs of Tacoma, Washington, near Mount Rainier. My family lived in a cul-de-sac in a small neighborhood full of parks and trees. For most of my early childhood, I played outside with my brother and the other neighborhood kids.

When I was in kindergarten, my teachers started to recognize that the way I wrote and learned was different from the other children. By the second grade, I was labeled as legally blind and in need of "special education." I was formally tested in middle school and discovered that I had dyslexia.

My parents were both entrepreneurs—my father a family physician who started a medical practice in the town nearby, and my mother who ran her own advertising agency out of our home. In our household, we frequently talked sex and money. Nothing was taboo.

After discovering my dyslexia, I learned how to advocate for myself to my teachers and colleagues. I excelled at the arts and hands-on learning. When I was ten years old, I made the best soccer team in the state, and I continued to play competitive soccer for the next seven years. Other players may have had more talent, but I worked hard, and I have been told that my role supporting team-building and cooperation led to group success in ways that exceeded my physical contributions.

After two years at the University of Portland in Oregon, I entered the business school after barely passing calculus. I tried marketing first but eventually declared a major in finance and accounting. My college mentor told me, "If you know finance, you can do anything in business. It may be the hardest major here, but you can do it!"

During my senior year of college, my mom was diagnosed with stage IV ovarian cancer. I moved home and finished most of my last semester of college remotely. My mother's illness was a key crisis for my family, a wake-up call to change our lifestyles. I realized I needed to live my life to the fullest.

I remember pushing back the start date for my first job as an accountant at Ernst & Young due to the economic collapse of 2008. During this forced sabbatical, I traveled the East Cape of Mexico, learning from people who were living off only solar energy. I learned to surf and sail and experienced my first *temazcal* (a type of sweat lodge) with a group of people indigenous to Mexico City. I remember talking to Jesse Ventura, the professional wrestler and former governor of Minnesota, who lived off the grid in Mexico. I asked him then, "Should I even start in the corporate world? Or should I find another way?"

I did start in the corporate world. The education system of labels and grades that I had grown up in had impacted my ability to think for myself and had created self-limiting beliefs. All my life up to this point, I had not been truly making my own decisions. Teachers, grades, my parents, my church, and society had all influenced me.

When I entered the working world, I set a goal for myself to learn from it—and then to become financially free before my thirties. I was called "hauditor" (hot auditor) by clients as I moved from one company to the next, learning the ins and outs. In all my jobs, I traveled all over the United States.

I met another accountant, and we dated for a few years. He proposed to me under the Eiffel Tower. In 2015, forty-five days before our wedding, we broke up. Afterwards, I decided to make major changes and essentially dismantled my life. I studied happiness and prepared to quit my job, saving money and researching future travels. I switched my honeymoon trip to Nicaragua and had a solo adventure in Central America.

At the beginning of 2016, I quit my job to pursue my solo travel dream. I traveled to Ireland to learn about my ancestors' traditions, see ancient sites, and experience the culture. Later that year, I visited France—another place of family heritage—and went wine-tasting through farms and villages. I frolicked in lavender fields and snorkeled in the South of France.

I then returned home to Washington and decided to hike as many mountains as possible, heading off on backpacking trips and discovering mystical lakes. I went to a ten-day Vipassana meditation center near Mount Saint Helens. I stopped making any decisions that were based on anything other than my intuition and heart.

At the end of 2016, I flew back to Mexico and started traveling through Central America, volunteering at different permaculture farms. Living as a volunteer, I had the opportunity to exchange my time for room and board. I studied Mayan culture and regenerative lifestyles with women-led food forests and cooperatives.

I met my partner, Alan, in Guatemala during Cosmic Convergence Festival in 2016. Together, we moved to Costa Rica in September of 2017 to follow our passion for regenerative living through action. We purchased a small piece of paradise with an old-growth food forest near Puerto Viejo in Limón. We set up a small office cabin and an edible botanical garden. We started teaching regenerative permaculture workshops. Then I met a dream community project, Jungle Project, which is all about trees, training, and trade through breadfruit-based community supply chain networks.

Additionally, I became a soil advocate for Kiss the Ground and got involved in local volunteer committees.

In 2019, Alan and I purchased a hectare (2.5 acres) in southern Costa Rica, setting up a full permaculture farm. We moved into this jungle paradise to develop our food sovereignty and live simply and holistically. The land already had an established home and many mature edible fruit trees growing on former pastureland. In 2020, lockdowns and border closures helped us stay focused on our mission, releasing us from "normal" distractions such as traveling, watching the news, or going out frequently.

I can count many, many experiences and lifetimes in the first thirty-four years of my life. I feel beyond blessed and grateful for all the perspectives and lessons along the way. Today, I am happy to be working for myself. Alongside Alan, I am on my way to sovereignty in water, food, and solar energy.

I couldn't be more proud to be who I am in the present: a holistic being and a lover of life. I still consider myself a forest fairy, too, just like I did when I was a little girl.

It is when I live my passions, work for myself, and embody love that I truly live to my fullest potential. Over the past years, I have shifted my perspective from survival mode to "thrival mode."

---

## THRIVAL MODE

When we live our dreams every day—satisfying our basic needs, cultivating self-love, and taking care of the earth and each other—we live with purpose. We paint each brushstroke with beautiful moments and cherish the simple pleasures.

---

This book is a memoir and a guide based on the tools that helped me regenerate my reality. It is my hope that it plants a seed of regeneration in your path, too.

## REGENERATE YOUR REALITY: THE BOOK

We are all full of magic. We are all forces of nature.

I have felt the call of environmentalism throughout my life. I want to leave the planet better than I found it— to leave it thriving for the generations to come.

### Mantra for Regeneration

*Action speaks.*

*Words must be impeccable.*

*Do the best you can.*

*Don't take anything personally.*

*FLY (First Love Yourself).*

*Serve others how you want to be treated.*

*Receive and give.*

*Listen to intuition.*

*Empower farmers.*

*Check in with your heart.*

*Follow your passions.*

*Protect this earth.*

*Stand as a steward of the lands.*

This book is about my personal journey, research, and life experiments. In it, I draw on teachers, books, and movies that have inspired me, as well as affirmations, prayers, journal entries, and stories. This book is not necessarily in chronological order. Much of my life has unfolded magically with spirals and infinite lessons, and the same is true for this book. Speaking of magic, I know that I was made from love, and I have created *Regenerate Your Reality* with the intention to spread it far and wide. I want to use my privilege and resources for the betterment of the communities I serve.

As I write this in 2020, the times feel apocalyptic. We have extracted so much from the earth and waters that our planet is out of balance. The climate is changing, but we still have time to restore ourselves and this earth. If we don't start to regenerate our world—in all ways—it is possible that most species will soon become extinct as biodiversity continues to decline. The global population has grown from 1 billion in 1800 to 7.8 billion in 2020. With that growth has come the development of agriculture and spaces for feeding and housing humans.[2] The unequal distribution of resources has divided the population in a struggle for survival.

In David Attenborough's environmental documentary, *A Life on Our Planet*, Attenborough concludes that

---

2 Max Roser, Hannah Ritchie, and Esteban Ortiz-Ospina, "World Population Growth," Our World in Data (Our World in Data, May 9, 2013), https://ourworldindata.org/world-population-growth.

biodiversity has degenerated before his eyes.[3] This film is his witness statement, attesting to the destruction he has observed in his own lifetime. In his more than sixty years working as a naturalist, Attenborough has mapped the loss of the planet's tropical forests at a rate of 37 million acres per year.

We are all part of the global climate solution. The climate crisis we are experiencing is also an opportunity for change—a call to connect with ourselves and our surroundings (our ecosystems). We can prevent irreparable damage to our planet. Earth, Gaia, Mother Nature is alive and conscious, and our bodies are an extension of her.

> "We showed that we are united and that we, young people, are unstoppable."
> —Greta Thunberg, UN Youth Climate Summit, New York City, September 21, 2019

Our planet has the capacity to provide all that is needed for those inhabiting it. We are meant to thrive with nature, co-creating life with harmony and love. According to Regeneration International, ecologists have discovered that planting more trees—1.2 trillion, to be exact—could neutralize carbon dioxide ($CO_2$) emissions on planet

---

3 Scholey, Keith, Hughes, Johnathan, and Alastair Fothergill, dirs. *David Attenborough: A Life on Our Planet,* Netflix Originals (September 28, 2020), https://www.netflix.com/title/80216393.

Earth.[4] The jungles and tropics are the lungs of this earth. They brought me and Alan to Costa Rica.

We came to plant trees and thrive, living off the abundance of the land, harvesting and producing our food as we dance through the gardens. We dreamt of agroforestry and edible forests replacing our broken conventional agricultural systems. We dreamt of being sovereign and making love to life.

We are witnessing the end of one chapter and the beginning of a new one. The death of patriarchal ways and the rise of ancestral solutions and community sovereignty. It is time to overhaul the way we live life.

We have the power to choose.

We are part of nature, and like nature we each have the potential for regeneration within us. Nature would heal itself if left untouched by humans. However, due to the extraction and destruction we have caused as a species, we must work with nature and *choose* to leave it better than we found it.

What transitions have you made? What are you doing to be the change you want to see? So many children of the earth, young and old, want to restore and love nature. So let's move away from empty talk—and toward collective action.

---

4 Ronnie Cummins and Andre Leu, "Best Practices: How Regenerative & Organic Agriculture and Land Use Can Reverse Global Warming," Regeneration International, April 7, 2021, https://regenerationinternational.org/2021/03/08/best-practices-how-regenerative-organic-agriculture-and-land-use-can-reverse-global-warming/.

This planet is our home. Our connection to the earth is related to everything else in our lives, and so this book offers suggestions to regenerate yourself, your communities, and the environment.

Regeneration is multifaceted, requiring change at all levels. The first step of regeneration begins with us, and then it ripples out to our communities and circles—and beyond. *Regenerate Your Reality* reflects my journey of change, and it is my hope that it will support you to follow your heart's path to regeneration.

---

## REGENERATION

Every live organism is capable of regeneration–from bacteria and soil to *floresta*, water, biodiversity, and humans. We love Kiss the Ground's definition: "Regeneration is more than a tool to sequester carbon. It's the path to honoring Indigenous wisdom and practices that will build resiliency and abundance for future generations."[5]

---

## STARTING YOUR JOURNEY

This book is one perspective—mine—and I encourage you to interpret it however you feel best. There are exercises and wisdom questions at the end of each chapter, which you can follow as you go or skip until later.

---

5 Kiss the Ground Facebook Post. @KisstheGround on March 1, 2021, https// x.facebook.com/kissthegroundCA/photos/a.506446989421998/37940116 33998834/?type=3.

*Do as you feel.*

*Move with your heart.*

This vast universe contains so much knowledge for us to tap into. Most of this knowledge is already taught, spoken, written, and within us; we just need to remember it.

We know everything and nothing. The only way forward is inward—journeying into our deepest depths. I invite you to discover what is true and intuitive to you. Study patterns of nature, start living with the cycles of your garden, and nurture a relationship with the soil.

Let's leave this earthship better than we found it.

## IDEAS FOR IMMEDIATE ACTION:

You don't even have to read the book first!

- Plant a garden—at home or in neighborhood schools, free spaces, or pots—indoors and outdoors.

- Buy local and organic as much as possible.

- Gain back your connection to the earth and your food. Start a compost pile! Get to know your farmers. Forage in the forest.

- Loving yourself means loving this planet. Get outside and spend time in the forest, fields, or desert.

- ⊚ Reducing your carbon footprint or becoming carbon neutral begins with a single step. Plant trees or support tree planting by donating!

- ⊚ Activate your dreams by living them through action.

- ⊚ Give back to your local communities.

"The only ethical decision is to take responsibility for our own existence and that of our children. Make it now."
—Bill Mollison

"A journey of a thousand miles begins with a single step."
—Lao Tzu

# I
# DREAMS

**Affirmation: I take action on my dreams every day.**

*"Since your 'dream come true' is original to you, it serves
as your creative contribution to the world. And it's when
you make an original contribution to the world that you
experience yourself as one with the world. The inner game is
making your true self an everyday reality."*

—Victoria, *Making Your Dream Come True*

∞

### 5/7/2018 Playa Chiquita, Costa Rica

*When I am love,*
*When I am joy,*
*Everything is effortless,*
*Flowing with universal energies.*
*I wake in the sunlight.*
*Snorkeling, I am taken to another universe.*
*Baptism by Mama Ocean.*
*A dimension of magic.*
*Another queendom of life: water forests.*
*Every action stems from the path of passion.*
*Today is the best day, and it's only the beginning.*
*Gratitude for all the love.*
*My spirit is back.*
*I am on my heart's path.*

∞

As I write today, I know I live my dream every single day. Freedom is a state of mind, a vibrant and holistic way of life. It is easier said than practiced. The freedom I'm talking about starts with loving ourselves, accepting ourselves, and liberating ourselves from limiting beliefs.

I used to think that freedom meant you had to struggle for abundance. I had to spend a painful amount of hours working for others to pay for my own apartment and meet all of my material needs. By my mid-twenties, I was working in the corporate world, traveling, attending glamorous events, leading financial trainings, and working with company executives. It was a dream job in most of my colleagues' minds, and it was for me as well—until my Saturn return.

---

## SATURN RETURN

The Saturn return occurs when the planet Saturn comes back to meet your natal Saturn. Our Saturn return happens every 27–29.5 years when this slow-moving planet returns to where it was when we were born. The Saturn return hits in the late twenties and late fifties. For those of us not following our hearts, the Saturn return is a wake-up call, surfacing sobering realities. When we are on our heart's path, then clarity and abundance are accelerated, and we feel affirmed in our lives.

---

## DISMANTLING

When I turned twenty-eight, I realized I was living a life that was out of alignment with my heart's path. Society, the media, and the education system had engraved a road in me at such an early age; it took me nearly thirty years to even consider any alternative. I wasn't thriving; I was in survival mode.

I was engaged to a man who proposed to me under the Eiffel Tower in France with a fancy diamond ring. We had a wedding coming up that I was allergic to planning, and we lived in a big home where we rented out the second unit. My fiancé and I had moved in together officially when we got engaged, and that was when I realized who he really was—a man with beliefs that were the extreme opposite of mine. I couldn't believe it. I didn't understand how I had gotten to this point.

How had we never touched these topics before? We lived a long-distance relationship, each with our own travels and jobs, seeing each other every other weekend for several years, meeting up in exotic spots like Hawaii or exploring glaciers in Alaska. I was one of his first girl-friends, and he pretty much agreed with me or had no comments for years—until we decided to talk about marriage, children, and core beliefs. I remember asking my pastor at the time, "Why does he take every word of the Bible literally?" My pastor replied, "It's like picking out one tree in the forest, instead of seeing the forest as love."

I realized that this in-depth communication should have come at the beginning of the relationship, but at that time I was still figuring out my path. My former fiancé and I grew up with different sets of beliefs that only surfaced as we moved deeper than our romantic getaways and weekend visits.

∞

### 3/1/2015 Seattle, Washington

*How can someone change their beliefs overnight?*
*What is the root of change? Or, if you felt that way for the last few years,*
*how did you hold those feelings in?*
*Why are we not being clear, strong, and transparent about what we believe?*

*It feels like a lie not to share our true values and beliefs until we get engaged. If this is caused by an event, then what other beliefs can change so drastically?*
*For the sake of pleasing someone? For the sake of having a beautiful woman by your side?*

*I want to be with someone who holds strong to what they believe, who lives their values. I have made my mistakes, but I believe that is why I'm here, now. I don't have regrets; I believe I learn and grow from the past.*

∞

I hit my Saturn return questioning everything: What is real? What is my heart's calling?

*How did I never really have depth in my relationship?*

*How did I not know who I was marrying?*

*How did I not know myself?*

The way the education system and the working world matrix were, I had never had time for myself beyond going into the woods for quick hikes or racing to yoga classes on lunch breaks or weekends. Of course, I had luxury vacations with friends, where we wine-tasted our way through the South of France, and vacation time with family. I thought I was living my dream, and then I realized that my dream was transforming into something different. Suddenly everything was up for questioning.

I didn't sleep for months due to the anxiety of not telling anyone how I was feeling and what was going on inside me. One way I could sleep was by watching a scene from *The Sound of Music*—"When the dog bites / when the bees sting / when I'm feeling sad . . ." I was enduring a dark phase of digging deep into questions, worrying about my mom's cancer, and feeling bored at my job. I was afraid of getting married, having realized that the lack of depth in my relationship was a mirror of myself. More importantly, I was starting to see that I needed to follow my deepest desires. I needed to follow my heart.

## I THOUGHT I NEEDED THERAPY, BUT REALLY I NEEDED TO FOLLOW MY HEART.

"For years, I worked a job that wasn't aligned with me—my goals, dreams, beliefs, desires, passions—and for years, I was unhappy.

I ignored this growing sense of dissatisfaction and continued working because I had to pay off my student loans.

I numbed it out and distracted myself with emotional eating, shopping, and overachieving.

The stress and nature of the work I was doing put me more in my masculine energy, and I became more disconnected from my sensuality and feminine energy (Shakti).

I felt completely turned off and disconnected from my body. I felt drained and depressed.

There came a point where I felt that my soul was dying. I felt stuck, unfulfilled, and unsatisfied.

I'd done all of the right things according to society. I had secured a "good" job and I had earned two advanced degrees, but still I was unhappy.

"There must be something wrong with me if I'm not happy," I thought.

So I reached out to a therapist and had a few appointments. In hindsight, now that I'm a coach, I can see that really all she did was coach me.

There was nothing wrong with me; I didn't need to work on any deep psychological issues. What I needed to do was find out what made me happy and do that instead.

Unfortunately, after a couple sessions, I wasn't able to continue seeing the therapist to get the support I needed to leave my job because of payment and insurance logistics. So I continued to stay stuck where I was, until one day (while in meditation during my training to become a yoga teacher), I received the clarity to finally break free from the trappings of so-called success, student loans, city living, and a nine-to-five "academic professional" career at a university that no longer served me.

I finally quit my job, followed my heart, returned to nature, and reconnected to my feminine energy. I stopped suppressing and sacrificing myself, reactivated Shakti, and reconnected to my creative life force energy. I had always wanted to travel and experience life outside of the Western world firsthand, but I hadn't had the courage to actually do it until that point.

It hadn't made logical sense to quit my job to travel because it wasn't a smart career choice or part of a clear path.

In hindsight, I can see that like most people, I was simply afraid of the uncertainty that following my heart would bring, which was stifling my growth and making me feel unhappy.

Deep down, I wanted to be free.

To connect to the wisdom of nature.
To live simply.
And in harmony.
So I did.

It took me a while to gain the clarity and courage necessary
to take the leap, but I finally did it.

I headed to the Caribbean coast of Costa Rica to teach yoga,
play on the beach, and live in the jungle, and I never looked
back.

Four years later, I'm ready to hold space for others who are
on a similar journey of freedom and self-discovery."

–Danielle Ashé, Multidimensional High Priestess
Co-author of Ancient-Future Unity: Reclaim Your Roots,
Liberate Your Lineage, Live a Legacy of Love[6]
@multidimensionalhighpriestess

All the answers came to me after my twenty-eighth birthday: I needed to walk the path less traveled. I needed to
go out on my own and travel solo.

---

6 Ashé Danielle and Jane Astara Ashley, *Ancient-Future Unity: Reclaim Your Roots,
Liberate Your Lineage, Live a Legacy of Love* (Old Saybrook, CT: Flower of Life Press,
2021).

∞

*10/19/2015 Seattle, Washington*

*Life is too short not to live it to its fullest. We are too young not to take risks and try different ways of living. I feel passion and excitement about traveling and living in other countries. I need greater flexibility with work and the freedom to work on my own terms.*

∞

## MY HEALING JOURNEY

The first book I read on my self-help journey was *The Mastery of Love* by Miguel Ruiz, and I continue to come back to it.

> "If you take your happiness and put it in someone's hands, sooner or later, she is going to break it. If you give your happiness to someone else, she can always take it away. Then if happiness can only come from inside of you and is the result of your love, you are responsible for your happiness."
> —Miguel Ruiz, *The Mastery of Love*

As I began dismantling my former life, a few girlfriends were my saving grace. We were all going through major transitions, and we supported each other through deconstructions and breakups. We created women's gatherings and moon ceremonies by the ocean and served as unofficial therapists for one another. At this point, I started to create my own rituals, which I still carry now. I journal and plant seeds with each new moon and full moon, writing out my goals, manifestations, and what I want to release and bring into my life. I connect with Mother Nature in a special celebration of life.

In 2015, after six months of anxiety, I finally made the decision to break up with my fiancé. A year later in 2016, I quit my secure job, sold all of my material possessions, and started to live my solo travel dream. I entered a realm of trust, flow, and "synchrodestiny." Changing my honeymoon trip to Nicaragua and Costa Rica, I set a small budget for myself and started traveling through Central America.

---

### SYNCHRODESTINY

A term coined by Deepak Chopra that describes a combination of synchronicity and destiny, a coincidence that occurs but with purpose and meaning and direction and intention. When we are in touch with synchrodestiny, we feel that we are divinely guided.

---

∞

*1/17/2017 Volcán Acatenango, Guatemala*
*Viewing the world from 13,045 feet*
*Only when we are no longer afraid do we begin to live.*

*Fire in the sky*
*Heating up my soul*
*Trembling below me*

*Exploding in front of me*
*Flowing beyond me*
*Smoking on the horizon*
*I am*

*We are at base camp when Volcán Fuego erupts as a fireworks show all night.*
*We are in wonderlust, hugging, crying, and kissing each other with excitement.*
*It has been almost a year since I left my life of working in the corporate world, making a steady paycheck, and living in one home. I left a life of materialism and capitalism in a quest to fill myself with joy, happiness, and peace.*
*Traveling, I soon realized I was never alone because I had an open heart. I was attracting people who would become lifelong friends, who saw the world through a different lens. People I would road-trip with, travel with for weeks, live with, cry with, kiss, and fall in love with. I turned off my phone and internet for weeks, connecting to the ocean, the mountains, and the lake, and I never felt greater joy.*
*This life is the life I choose, outside with nature. Healing myself through food and meditation. Crying and feeling anytime it is necessary. Letting out energy that doesn't serve me. Filling myself up with self-love each day. Falling more in love with life each moment.*

*Climbing Volcán Acatenango was one of the highlights of my year, pushing me so far beyond my comfort zone.*

∞

"True self-discovery begins where your comfort
zone ends."

—Adam Braun

## DREAM LIFE

Happiness is not a destination; it is a way of life. Traveling
solo, I entered a "thrival mode"—the opposite of survival
mode—of creating my own reality.

In case you need a reminder of what thrival mode
looks like, here is my definition:

---

### THRIVAL MODE

When we live our dreams every day–satisfying our basic needs,
cultivating self-love, and taking care of the earth and each other–we
live with purpose. We paint each brushstroke with beautiful moments
and cherish the simple pleasures.

---

As I started to go inward and assess each aspect of my
life, I understood what was real and what was illusory.
I followed my heart through Central America, and I
thought I would make it all the way down to Patagonia,
but I found my home in Costa Rica instead.

Just because we are born somewhere doesn't mean
we can't migrate. Our dreams and outlooks evolve as we
grow and learn about the world. When our dreams and
perspectives evolve and grow, sometimes we need a different environment to contain them.

Our dreams and goals ebb and flow with the cycles of life. They can change in an instant when we wake up from the "fog" of social conditioning or from familial expectations, and start to find our own way.

---

### FOG

Fog, as the Toltec teach, describes the state of living in an illusion, feeling separate, and suffering from not measuring up to what we are supposed to be. We're trained to unquestioningly adopt certain beliefs and values, which may not be conducive to our well-being, nor to the well-being of our society or the planet.

---

## WHERE I AM NOW

Today, I am realizing another dream of living off the land, planting edible food forests, working on collaborative regeneration projects, living with my lover, and meeting my basic needs without having to work for anyone else. I believe we must live our dreams each day, redesigning them to our heart's fancy whenever necessary.

If we don't act on our own dreams and passions, we may easily become stuck in fog, depression, or dis-ease. We can become depressed when the woes of the world are compounded by our inaction—when we are not doing anything that sets our soul on fire or gets us excited to wake up every morning.

"Any action is often better than no action, especially if you have been stuck in an unhappy situation for a long time. If it is a mistake, at least you learn something, in which case it's no longer a mistake. If you remain stuck, you learn nothing. It is not uncommon for people to spend their whole life waiting to start living." —Eckhart Tolle, *The Power of Now: A Guide to Spiritual Enlightenment*

I have had so many different dreams that I catch and release, only to realize that they weave into even more dreams, too magical and joyful to describe. It is so important to allow ourselves time and space to get to know ourselves as individuals, to dig deep into our patterns and our discomforts, and to discover our multifaceted passions and talented selves. In my process of self-discovery, I realized that spending most of my time inside a building, sitting in front of a screen, and working for others was not my calling.

"Life is nothing but a dream, and if we are artists, then we can create our life with Love, and our dream becomes a masterpiece of art." —Miguel Ruiz, *The Mastery of Love*

My dreams changed as I grew and learned—evolving from my childhood dreams to the dreams of my early twenties and then to the dreams I have today. Sometimes our deepest beliefs can change, and we become open to new opportunities our minds couldn't once comprehend. Perhaps we reach all of our dreams and goals, and then we still keep dreaming, living in the present, and believing that everything is possible.

## MAYBE YOU HAVEN'T EVEN DREAMED IT YET!

"We often talk about making our dreams come true. The sky's the limit, that kind of thing.

But, going out on a limb here, what about the things we never dared to dream? What about the possibilities that didn't even enter into our orbit of awareness? What if the sky isn't the limit?

I've had a lot of conversations recently about the gnarled, labyrinthine trails we call our life path.

I didn't dream up this life; I lived it into existence, one day at a time. In fact, I couldn't have dreamed it even if I'd tried! So many key ingredients hadn't come into my path yet.

I think it's great to have goals and aspirations. They keep us focused and challenge us to grow. However, I would argue that when we limit (yes, limit) ourselves *only* to what we can dream, two things happen:

1. We dream small, because we are scared to dream too big. I notice this in myself all the time as I envision new projects. Why do you think it took me so long to write my book? A

travel blog was an "achievable" dream. But a book . . . What if I failed? Or worse, what if I succeeded?!

2. We don't know what we don't know. I can't plan a future full of people I haven't met yet, experiences I have yet to live, and information I haven't yet learned. I can only set goals that exist within the realm of conscious possibility. But what about all the possibilities I can't even imagine?

Ten years ago, I never would have imagined the life I have today. Today, I know that I have *no idea* what my life will look like ten years from now. The people, places, ideas, and projects that will populate it–maybe I haven't even met them yet. I certainly haven't dreamed them."

–Toby Israel,[7] Author of *Vagabondess*,
Founder of Mujeres Fuertes
@mujeresfuertescostarica
@vagabondesstravel

---

7 "Be Happy. Be Free. Vagabond.," Toby Israel (Toby Israel LLC, February 12, 2019), http://www.tobyisrael.me/.

# Guided Inquiry

**Intro written by Astaria Light[8], Founder of Light of Sound, Sound Alchemist and Voice Midwife @lightofsound**

"Sometimes the hardest thing is simply showing up for our dreams.

With all the things we constantly have going on, it can feel challenging to make time and space for what seems less urgent.

Our dreams and creative endeavors can take a backseat as we prioritize seemingly more important life things.

When we are stuck in survival mode, we can neglect things that don't seem to put food on the table.

But what if you could reframe the way you approach your creative dreams and realize that they absolutely are important for your thrival on this planet?

An act of devotion to your creative muses can simply look like five to thirty minutes a day of honoring your connection with something beyond your day-to-day responsibilities.

The feminine desires to have a voice, to be seen and heard, to express herself. And when we are not following our passions, we can feel stagnant and depressed about

---

8 Light of Sound Temple (astaria light of sound), accessed November 2, 2021, https://www.lightofsound.com/.

life. We seem to lose our vigor and inspiration for the magic of what life can share when we don't dance with our muses.

To show up, regardless of all the reasons not to, is an act of devotion.
And the more we show up, the more we create a new groove in our life—and a new habit and path start to take form.
We invite in a breath of fresh air, and inspiration starts to flow again. We remember who we are and find clarity around our purpose.
Sometimes we forget . . . only to remember and find our way again.
It's never too late to start something new.
*So, what is one thing that you always seem to dream about but have been putting off?*
*Will you show up in devotion to this dream, even if for just five minutes a day?*
S/he yearns for your connection and presence."

## Inspiring Change

What are the priorities, dreams, or goals in your life? One of the greatest feelings is knowing that we are constantly improving, learning, growing, and thriving. We need to check in on ourselves regularly to get there.

Be sure to take time to feel, reflect on, and really evaluate each area in your life. Then, in your journal, rate from one to ten how each of the following shows up in your life—one being the least to ten being the most—and write notes under each category:

- ☺ Health
- ☺ Business / Career
- ☺ Spirit / Soul
- ☺ Finance
- ☺ Relationships—with Self / Earth / Others (including Family or Partner)
- ☺ Creativity
- ☺ Adventure / Fun
- ☺ Romance
- ☺ Giving Back / Community Service

# Inspiring Action

## FLY (FIRST LOVE YOURSELF)

We can fill ourselves up with love, gratitude, devotion, and fun so that our love overflows and ripples out to serve our communities and the earth. When we love ourselves first, then we can fully show up in our lives to live regeneration in every way.

*Based on your self-assessment above, what areas can you improve?*

*What new habit could you adopt to thrive more?*

Set a new twenty-one-day habit (new food choices, new disciplines, etc.), and stick to it! The twenty-one- and ninety-day rules[9] state that it takes twenty-one days to make something a habit and ninety days to make it a permanent lifestyle change. That's a short period of time to experiment with yourself and try to reprogram your thoughts, patterns, and disciplines.

Over the next twenty-one days, track your new habit(s) with gratitude and self-compassion. Each day, spend time in nature by going on a walk in the forest, sitting under a tree, or visiting your favorite water spot. Give yourself a

---

9 "21/90 Good Habits and a Great Life," Active Iron, June 25, 2020, https://www.activeiron.com/blog/the-21-90-rule-make-life-better/.

few minutes to connect with your breath and your deepest desires. As you begin to regenerate your body, mind, and spirit, ponder these wisdom questions:

## Wisdom Questions

- ♥ What dreams and desires are surfacing?

- ♥ Am I searching for more, or am I satisfied with everything in the present?

- ♥ What triggers are arising, and what are the roots?

# II
# PASSION PATH

**Affirmation: I make my dream my reality through my actions and passions. I follow the call of my heart and intuition.**

*"Walk and touch peace every moment.*
*Walk and touch happiness every moment.*
*Each step brings a fresh breeze.*
*Each step makes a flower bloom.*
*Kiss the Ground with your feet.*
*Bring the Earth your love and happiness.*
*The Earth will be safe*
*when we feel safe in ourselves."*

—Thich Nhat Hanh

"If you inherently long for something, become it first. If you want gardens, become the gardener. If you want love, embody love. If you want mental stimulation, change the conversation. If you want peace, exude calmness. If you want to fill your world with artists, begin to paint. If you want to be valued, respect your own time. If you want to live ecstatically, find the ecstasy within yourself. This is how to draw it in, day by day, inch by inch."

—Victoria Erickson

∞

### 4/6/2020 Pacific Hills, Costa Rica

*Life is so blessed.*
*We predicted these global events of*
*crisis and fragile systems.*

*There is so much uncertainty.*

*I believe Mother Earth and the universe have a divine plan.*
*Respecting and treating all with love, honoring Mother*
*Nature—*
*in my world, magic is flowing.*
*Fish kissing me. Double rainbows shining. Slow cooking.*
*Savoring life. Enjoying. Dancing. Singing.*
*We are meant to thrive.*

*I have a deep compassion for those who are living*
*in a box*
*—of controlled air, processed food, and watching a box.*

*I feel so delighted cultivating love,*
*propagating plants, and regenerating lands.*

**Thank you, God, for the visions,**
*for the magical synchronicities*
*that brought me to this path.*

∞

As I traveled through Central America, I learned some truths that continue to set my passion on fire. I learned that we can channel our fire and anger to create change and take action. While traveling, I followed my heart and achieved my goals to complete my yoga teacher training, volunteer on a permaculture farm, and learn Spanish.

I didn't know what my service to the world would be, but I just continued to trust my heart as I followed my passion path. As a volunteer at Mystical Yoga Farm in Guatemala, I traded my time and work in exchange for a portion of my yoga teacher training. While there, I practiced yoga and learned how to grow my own food all while living on less than fifty dollars a week. Volunteer or work-trade agreements can be excellent opportunities to practice your passions in exchange for most of your living costs.

During my travels, I started to recognize that part of my calling is to embody environmentalism in my lifestyle. I saw firsthand how capitalism devastated communities. I saw how greed for money and resources won out at the expense of people's livelihoods, land, and water. I saw how people in the so-called "third world" were living in community and sharing resources. People were living off of very little income and still seemed happy. Why? Because they were meeting their basic needs for food, water, shelter, and community.

Below are a few learnings from my travel journals describing the moments when I began to see my calling take shape in the fire I was feeling:

∞

## 2/2/2017 El Paredon, Guatemala

*In Mayan culture, mountains are guardians of the land.*
*Mayans believe God is in everything around them.*
*As a greeting, Mayans ask, "¿Cómo está tu corazón?" (How is*
*your heart?)*
*How beautiful is this culture?*
*It is eye-opening to see the perspectives of the locals on*
*capitalism and its devastating effects on their communities*
*and land. We only have one life, one earth.*
*We are all one.*
*Protect it.*

∞

"The history of Latin America is the history of the development of world capitalism. Our defeat was always implicit in another's victory. Our wealth has always generated poverty in order to feed the prosperity of others: the empires and their cronies. In colonial and neocolonial alchemy, the gold transforms into scrap iron, and the food converts to poison." —*Sipakapa No Se Vende,*[10] a documentary about Goldcorp mining on Mayan land

I love studying and learning about Mayan culture. When I lived in Guatemala, I studied Spanish in Antigua, realizing my goal of being able to communicate with the

10 Caracol Producciones, "Sipakapa No Se Vende (Subtítulos Inglés)." *YouTube* video, 56:17. April 4, 2014. https://youtu.be/F36SqLpqQmQ.

locals. I was inspired by the women protecting vibrant traditions and customs and tending to their food forests and I wanted to be able to converse with and learn from them. I toured many family gardens and saw how the only items they purchased were rice and beans; all the rest was grown in small spaces for cultivation.

∞

### 5/25/2017 *Tulum, Mexico*

*History repeats itself over and over.*
*Dehumanizing other cultures.*
*Using people.*
*Killing civilizations.*
*Converting indigenous cultures to organized religions.*
*"Gentrification."*
*War.*
*Destroying Mother Nature.*
*Taking, taking, taking.*
*Mines, energy, oil, trees.*
*Monoculture crops.*
*Chemical pesticides.*
*Pollution.*

∞

As Alan and I traveled through Mexico, I realized that certain parts of Mexico are extensions of the global capitalist system—fancy hotels and shops built for the benefit of luxury vacationers. Other areas of Mexico had ancient ruins that became Disney-style parks, attracting even more consumption and pollution with herds of people walking through.

∞

### 6/19/2017 Chichén Itzá, Mexico

*The Mayans led the way with mathematics, time, astronomy, and calendars.*
*For thousands of years, people have been asking questions about the universe.*
*The purpose of life.*
*History has continued to repeat itself in each society and culture:*
*A need for more resources.*
*More power.*

*We are the solution—and the problem.*
*We can choose to use our resources to regenerate land—or to destroy it.*
*We can vote for brands and plastic—or not.*

*We make a choice.*
*We have the solution.*
*We are it.*

∞

A fire ignited my call to action. I needed to begin living the change I wanted to see in the world. I could no longer just have an opinion and be angry.

## REGENERATION

The biggest gift is time. If we can start working for ourselves, in community, and become stewards of the symphony of life on this planet, then we can be free, abundant, and happy. Our micro-universe mirrors our outer-universe. In other words, we cultivate our inner garden along with the garden that surrounds us. It's a beautiful paradise home in my heart. What about yours?

As we continually regenerate ourselves and the planet, we actively create the harmony we wish to see. Each of us has unique offerings and magic to bring forth. When we drop into a state of "being," releasing all labels, titles, and professions, we become co-creators of life with everything around us.

In case you need a reminder of what regeneration is, here is my favorite explanation:

---

### REGENERATION

Every live organism is capable of regeneration–from bacteria and soil to *floresta*, water, biodiversity, and humans. We love Kiss the Ground's definition, "Regeneration is more than a tool to sequester carbon. It's the path to honoring Indigenous wisdom and practices that will build resiliency and abundance for future generations."[11]

---

11 Kiss the Ground Facebook Post. @KisstheGround on March 1, 2021, https://x.facebook.com/kissthegroundCA/photos/a.506446989421998/37940 11633998834/?type=3.

**What does regeneration of the body look like?** It means purifying our vessel (the body) with pure waters, organic foods, regular exercise, sleep, and rest. It means taking wellness days when needed. We restore the life force within when we get "high" on healthy activities that make us feel alive.

**What does regeneration of the earth look like?** It means to compost our organic materials, to plant seeds with the cycles, to tend to our gardens, to steward our lands, and to vote with our consumption.

Implementing the 7 R's is a great step toward regeneration in every way!

The following is my take on the 7 R's of regeneration.

- Rethink
- Refuse
- Reuse
- Repair
- Recycle
- Repurpose
- Regenerate!

When I became fed up with plastics and other wasteful patterns of consumption, I began my journey to **zero waste**. Along the way, I started to rethink what is really possible when it comes to regeneration at the individual level. Based on my ongoing regeneration journey, I've created the following guiding questions to help you think about the 7 R's[12] in your life.

- ◎ **Rethink**: What are the environmental consequences of what you eat, drink, purchase, and do? What effects do these activities have on yourself and the planet? Who are you working for and what is their intention?

  What are you shopping for? Consider buying secondhand, borrowing from your neighbor, or dumpster diving. Where do you spend your resources?

  Are you supporting local families and small business owners? Try and avoid mass consumerism and shop at local farmers' markets. Set up trading circles with your friends and in your community for books, clothes, and other household items you are not utilizing.

  Where does your food come from? Do you know its source? The source is not the supermarket. It's the soil and water that determine the quality of the food you buy.

---

12 "What Can You Do? the 7 R's: Rethink-Refuse-Reduce-Re-Choose-Repair-Reuse-Recycle," Oceanpreneur, February 16, 2021, https://www.theoceanpreneur.com/entrepreneurship/what-can-you-do-rethink-refuse-reduce-re-choose-reuse-recycle/.

Rethink your groceries and your diet. How much waste do you generate each week? What is it? How was your food produced? Our current agricultural model is extractive, while regenerative agriculture works to build topsoil, nourish the environment, draw down and sequester carbon, and bring back health and wealth to communities.

## Why regenerative agriculture?

- Builds and feeds the soil
- Compost or heavy mulch covers crops
- Holistic management
- Many yields and companion planting
- Supports healthy ecosystems
- Zero or minimal tilling
- Sequesters carbon
- Chemical-free
- Cooperates with nature

## Why not conventional agriculture?

- Depletes soil and is extractive to the environment
- Heavy use of toxic fertilizers
- Reductionist

- Plants in mono crops
- Creates dead zones, poisonous waterways, and desertification
- Relies on chemicals for high yields
- Attempts to beat and conquer nature

"If governments won't solve the climate, hunger, health, and democracy crises, then the people will. Regenerative agriculture provides answers to the soil crisis, the food crisis, the health crisis, the climate crisis, and the crisis of democracy."

—Dr. Vandana Shiva

- **Refuse**: An easy action we can take is to refuse single-use plastic and refuse to shop firsthand or at big-box supermarkets. We can purchase from local farmers' markets, make our own all-purpose cleaning products with vinegar and a few drops of peppermint essential oil, and make our own vinegar with fruit scraps (see recipe in Chapter 7). Consider using coconut oil in bulk for your skincare and cooking, and try not washing your hair every day to use less shampoo.

- **Reduce**: We can reduce our purchases of unnecessary products from large stores and instead grow our own gardens, trade for products or services, and exchange with our local community centers or colleagues.

◎ **Reuse**: Plastic can take around 450 years[13] to decompose. Single-use plastic items are great—for the companies that produce them. Fortunately, there's a reusable purpose for nearly every single-use thing out there! I prefer to refuse plastic, and I opt for purchasing specialty items in glass so that I can reuse the jars.

◎ **Repair**: Develop your handywoman skills and try to fix whatever breaks. Or if it's out of your league, see if there is an easy solution online (i.e., Google it), or hire an expert to repair it. Things are designed to go obsolete so that we continue to be ravenous consumers. But there are regenerative alternatives. A lot of stuff can be repaired, patched, or fixed up to extend their lives. When you absolutely need to purchase "new," do your homework and go for quality and repairability over price.

◎ **Recycle**: Recycle whatever is recyclable. Learn about your municipality's recycling policy and systems. If they offer compost bins, awesome, but I highly recommend composting at home if you

---

13 "How Long Does It Take for Plastic to Decompose?," Pela (Pela Case, March 9, 2020), https://pelacase.com/blogs/news/does-plastic-degrade#:~:text=Given%20 the%20resistant%20nature%20of,to%20decompose%20in%20a%20landfill.

have even a tiny yard or bringing your compost to a local organic community garden. Consider composting as the most eco-friendly way to recycle food waste and nourish our earth—building better soil.

- ⦿ **Repurpose:** Make your old clothes into rags, breathable coverings for fermentation, or vests.[14] Or upcycle items you're not using into art, turning trash into creations. My grandma, Fay Colmar, showed me how to make plastic into painted flower sculptures, for example.[15]

- ⦿ **Regenerate:** Regenerate in all ways. We must take steps toward our dreams by contributing to the betterment of our ecosystems. We can be part of making our home planet better than we found it. Regenerate your love for yourself and your relationship with Mother Earth. Regenerate your grass into edible gardens, build soil health, and compost. Restore your health and peace of mind.

---

14 Colmar, Mary. Vests. Upcycle. saladbowldress.com.
15 Margherita Beale , "At 87, Artist Fay Colmar Has an Exhibit at Cal State Fullerton and Can't Wait to Get Back to Work," Los Angeles Times (California Times, June 18, 2017), https://www.latimes.com/socal/daily-pilot/news/tn-wknd-et-bloody-marys-art-20170618-story.html.

## ZERO WASTE

Waste can be defined as something that doesn't have a use. The "zero waste" movement is about finding a use for everything. Focusing on waste prevention, the zero waste movement encourages the redesign of resource life cycles so that all products are reused, closing the loop and ultimately decomposing into the earth.

I believe zero waste requires, first and foremost, an empowering shift in mentality. In opening our mind to new ways of living and regenerating, we learn to challenge the status quo and tread our own path to happiness.

## CIRCULAR ECONOMY

As we think about old, linear systems of production—"take/consume," "throw away," and "out of sight, out of mind"—it is clear how this way of life pollutes the earth, leaving it much worse than we found it. Plastic, for example, takes decades to break down and even then continues to release microplastics and toxins into the environment. A circular economy creates closed cycles of production and promotes waste management with each product we consume.

## CIRCULAR ECONOMY IS BASED ON THREE PRINCIPLES:[16]

- ◎ Eliminate waste and pollution from production systems.

16 Liam Taylor, "Three Core Principles of the Circular Economy," Planet Ark, October 21, 2020, https://planetark.org/newsroom/news/three-core-principles-of-the-circular-economy.

⊚ Keep products and materials in use as long as possible.

⊚ Regenerate natural systems.

"The circular economy is a model of production and consumption, which involves sharing, leasing, reusing, repairing, refurbishing and recycling existing materials and products as long as possible . . . . In practice, it implies reducing waste to a minimum. When a product reaches the end of its life, its materials are kept within the economy wherever possible. These can be productively used again and again, thereby creating further value."

—European Parliament[17]

In a circular economy, activity builds and regenerates itself. Regeneration is about the entire cycle of life—from life to death. Nature works in cycles, circles, and spirals. Linear systems go against that natural order.

I am still on my journey to zero waste, and I get frustrated when everything is wrapped in plastic at stores. So, I try to boycott going to grocery stores as much as I can. I am happy to compost my food scraps. In our household, we produce one to three gallons of food scraps per day because we eat primarily from local farmers and our garden. Even our poop is reused! We have a "humanure"

---

17 "Circular Economy: Definition, Importance and Benefits: News: European Parliament," News | European Parliament, March 3, 2021.

compost toilet that enables this precious waste to return to the land to fertilize our fruit trees after two years, during which time it safely decomposes back into soil.

Our family uses eco-bricks, too. We push all our plastic waste into bottles (I like to use an empty gallon container from our laundry detergent), which become plastic-filled "bricks" we can then use to build structures. We consume our own crops, which then become poop, which we compost for two years before giving it back to the earth to nourish another cycle of food production.

Circular economy is not just a big concept for governments and economists, but something real that we can immediately put into practice as individuals.

## PASSION PATHS

Another passion path of mine is planting seeds and propagating plants with the full moon and new moon in any garden where I find myself residing. I plant seeds with the full moon and prune and cut back plants during the new moon. Now I live on a farm with hundreds of edible *perennials*, fruit trees, a greenhouse, and chickens. We are currently in a process of transitioning to complete food sovereignty.

---

## PERENNIALS[18]

All flowering plants have similar life cycles. Annual plants finish their life cycles in one growing season and need to be planted again the following season, whereas perennials live on for many years. Here in the tropics, perennials help us to be more efficient with our time, as they grow in two summer seasons each year: dry season and wet season. Many perennials can be propagated by a cutting, which makes it fun to reproduce abundance. Perennial plants are companions to fruit trees in a food forest.

---

Gardening is just one of many passions for me. I believe that we can be multi-passionate, holistic beings. Malcolm Gladwell's *Outliers: The Story of Success* explains that practicing our passions for ten thousand hours (per the "Ten Thousand-Hour Rule") is the key to success in any field. This could mean dedicating all our time to a single passion, or it could be years of devotion to and practice of several skills. I have a handful of diverse practices that I follow every day, such as yoga, herbalism, gardening, harvesting, fermentation, cooking, art, entrepreneurship, writing, and singing.

I have also gotten involved in regenerative community projects, like Jungle Project, that support local food production. Alan and I joined the road committee to ban chemical pesticides in our neighborhood, too, and we put

---

18 Balogh Anne, "Annual Vs Perennial – What Is the Difference?" *Garden Design Magazine.* https://www.gardendesign.com/annuals/vs-perennials.html.

a sign on our road saying *No Chemical Pesticides* with the regulation number. The region we live in, Pérez Zeledón, is the first zone in Costa Rica to ban chemical pesticides in public areas or roads. (Sadly, Costa Rica is the highest user of chemical pesticides per acre in the world.)[19]

## PERMACULTURE

As I traveled, I lived in many different communities with different lifestyles. I discovered permaculture as a missing link of connection for me and a possible solution to many of the world's problems. Permaculture philosophy is based on ancient agricultural practices and traditions of living in harmony with the earth.

"Permaculture is a powerful holistic tool for designing conscious relationships with everything that surrounds us—Mother Nature, plants, animals, human communities, and all energy that flows in our lives. Our ancestors were using some of these tools to thrive. We can also use these tools to restore Mother Nature and society from the effects of human destruction."

–Alan Cacao, Engineer, Biodynamics and Permaculture Teacher

In 2017, Alan and I visited Las Cañadas, where Alan lived for two years in his early twenties, learning, building with natural materials, and teaching permaculture. Las

19 Laura Alvarado, "Costa Rica Takes First Place in the World for the Use of Pesticides," Costa Rica Star News (The Costa Rica Star, May 3, 2018), https://news.co.cr/costa-rica-takes-first-place-in-the-world-for-the-use-of-pesticides/72749/.

Cañadas is a beautiful example of a cooperative permaculture project that has been thriving for over ten years. While there, I saw how necessary it is for us to transition to cooperatives and regenerative living.

---

## COOPERATIVES

Cooperatives are an organization of groups or persons working toward a common goal, which could be a farm, network, or project. They are jointly owned and operated and share benefits and proceeds. Typically, cooperatives have a strong commitment to serve their community's economic, cultural, and social needs. People and organizations using a cooperative model of shared ownership often apply permaculture principles: fair share, earth care, and people care.

---

I have learned about **permaculture** by living it at many different regenerative centers, volunteering, and taking hands-on courses. Now my partner and I have created our own 2.5-acre permaculture example, "Fairy Farm" (*Finca de las Hadas*).

## PERMACULTURE

The word "permaculture" was coined by Australian permaculturists Bill Mollison and David Holmgren in the mid-1970s. In its early days, permaculture was described as the "development of a permanent culture to create a foundation of supporting human needs based in harmony with nature. This foundation is rooted in the natural development of surplus or regeneration in your community and environment, rather than settling for sustainability."[20]

Las Cañadas, located in Veracruz, Mexico, is a cooperative permaculture project with 306 hectares (756 acres) of conservation land and agroforestry serving twenty-one associates and one hundred family members. (You can watch the full video about Las Cañadas on the Regenerate Your Reality website.)[21] It produces all its own resources and is a great example of a completely regenerative project. Las Cañadas is surrounded by other conscientious neighbors who were attracted to the community; today they partake in different activities and attend workshops on-site.

∞

*6/16/2017 Las Cañadas, Mexico*
*Living in the clouds,*
*where magic happens.*

20 Bill Mollison, *Permaculture: A Designers' Manual* (Tagari Publications, 1988).
21 Tropical Regeneration. "The Best Example Of Living Permaculture - Las Cañadas - Bosque De Niebla." *YouTube* video, 21:04. https://youtu.be/SgSjkdwN9io.

*The sun powers all.*
*The rain is collected.*
*The earth is formed into hobbit houses.*
*Bamboo into shelter.*
*Corn is sacred.*
*Plants fuel the temple.*
*Life is simple.*
*Living off the grid I feel more connected than ever.*

∞

Permaculture focuses on creating solutions through our actions. Permaculture is about noticing the patterns of nature around us and within us. Through it, we can come to know the rhythm of our bodies and the moon. It teaches us to know when we need time for reflection and when we need our community, our tribe.

## EMPOWERMENT THROUGH PERMACULTURE

"Permaculture is a tool for empowerment, offering people and communities a way back to once-commonplace ways of living and sustaining, and in some cases, thriving. At one time, each and every person knew survival strategies–where to forage and hunt for their food, which plants were medicines or poisons, how to find and collect water, where and how to construct shelter, how to make and mend their own clothing, and how to live with the seasons of the planet. Permaculture serves as a bridge for bringing people not only back to the land but back to their human nature, that is, as extensions of Earth–beings on the interconnected web of life.

Permaculture is the opposite of the Cartesian philosophical belief system that the world is a machine and a reservoir of resources for the human-machine to consume. Permaculture believes in a reciprocal and mutually beneficial relationship with the land and natural systems, which offer back as much as the human takes. It is the role of the human being to facilitate and guard over the natural biological and geological systems by being active participants, not bystanders, victims, or ravenous consumers."

–Sarah Marie Wu (Village Witch[22] @villagewitch.sarahwu,
Co-founder of Ecology Academy @ecologyacademy),
Co-founder of Envision

## CONCLUSION: PASSION PATH

The relationship between the earth, community, and nature reflects our relationship with ourselves. There are always more improvements and changes to come, but can we be happy exactly where we are and be proud of ourselves for that?

When we seek *more, more, more,* we lose sight of the journey, the pleasure of the ride. Our goal could be to get a little stronger each day and take lessons from life itself. Some days will be harder, and other days, we will float in bliss. We know that we are perfectly imperfect and constantly growing, evolving, and healing. We are *whole*, just how we are!

---

22 Village Witch, https://villagewitch.org/.

One of our most exciting blessings is the power of choice. We choose what to eat, drink, wear, accept, say, do, make, and buy. We choose with whom we work, play, converse, dance, and date.

With a plenitude of options in everything, it's sometimes difficult to make an intentional choice these days. As you consciously consume foods, clothing, and other retail products, ask yourself: Is your choice a great one for you, your family, and the planet? If you are unsure about the environmental consequences of your actions and lifestyle choices—research, discover, learn, unlearn, dig—and then choose.

Our capitalist-industrialist society shapes us into specialists. It creates a world where everything is linear, but this goes against nature's cyclicality. We can be multi-passionate and holistic in our lives. We are artists of each moment; we create our own reality with each thought, each word, and each action.

To regenerate my reality, I love entering a state of "being"—not planning anything and just getting into my creative flow or divine inspiration. Starting with self-love, gratitude, grounding, gardening, pure water, and fresh fruit, I tune into what my heart desires. I also love days where I have more structure and commitments. Life is a constant dance, flowing between masculine and feminine energies. Most of the time, I feel my day is perfectly full of diverse and vibrant activities.

When you find your passion, it attracts abundance. When we embody a state of love and thriving, we attract that back to us. In *Big Magic: Creative Living Beyond Fear*, Elizabeth Gilbert describes this creative process as having a romance with your passion:

> "Do whatever brings you to life, then. Follow your own fascinations, obsessions, and compulsions. Trust them. Create whatever causes a revolution in your heart."
> —Elizabeth Gilbert, *Big Magic: Creative Living Beyond Fear*[23]

My passion path is regeneration in every way—through mind, body, environment, and community. I believe that if enough of us take small actions, that effort magnified by millions can create real change in this world at a time when we need it most.

### *Prayer for Remembering*

*Allow us to remember that we are children of God, of this earth.*
*Allow us to treat all with unconditional love, protecting and planting seeds,*
*renewing, decomposing, and blooming again.*
*Just like the sun, we rise again,*

---

23 Elizabeth Gilbert, *Big Magic: Creative Living Beyond Fear* (New York, NY: Riverhead Books, 2016).

*setting with the moon as we remember our essence and*
*pureness.*
*Allow us to step up as stewards of this earth, making*
*change through each of our actions.*
*Let these collective actions*
*ripple,*
*catching fire,*
*and burning down old ways.*

# Guided Inquiry

## DRAGON DREAMING

### Intro written by Alan Cacao,[24]

"Dragon dreaming is a fantastic tool for manifestation—individual or collective—involving four simple steps that always connect in cycles. This practice helps to organize and support an organic process of manifesting our dreams into reality. We must always start by searching for clarity with our dreams, planning intelligently, acting and implementing, celebrating, growing, and then starting again the next cycle."

---

24 "Our Team," Regenerate Your Reality (Regenerate Your Reality, 2021), https://www.regenerateyourreality.com/team.

The **Dragon Dreaming**[25] process has at its foundation the interplay between individual and collective dreams.

While they were both working for the Gaia Foundation of Western Australia, John Croft and his late wife, Vivienne Elanta, created the Dragon Dream model. Dragon Dreaming relates our dreams to ecological processes, human processes, and indigenous traditions, as well as other social and environmental theories. The dragon dream is based on three key components: personal growth, community building, and service to the earth.

The four stages—dreaming, planning, doing, and celebrating—are not rigidly separated and are fractal in nature, as each stage involves all four stages within itself. In the dreaming stage, you begin with awareness, move to motivation, and then move to information gathering before crossing the threshold through celebration to the planning stage, again with its own four stages.

## CREATE YOUR OWN DRAGON DREAM

When Alan and I wanted to manifest our dream land together, we used this model to get clear on our needs and vision. Start with Dreaming and Planning, then move to Doing, and lastly, Celebrating. It is important to be as detailed as possible in all steps. Visit the Regenerate Your Reality website and search for our Dragon Dream post to start your journey.

---

25 "Dragon Dreaming," Dragon Dreaming International, accessed November 2, 2021, https://dragondreaming.org/.

# Free Your Voice!

As we pave our passion paths through dragon dreaming, it's so important to express ourselves freely. When we connect to our authentic voice, our dreams can really shine. What is sitting inside me that I need to put into words? Our inner voice and outward expressions are connected. Our voice is our truth.

How can I free myself from the fear of uncertainty, heaviness, and energy blockages? Our voice is our tool toward liberation from the inside out.

What are my hopes for this new world? How do I voice them? Let's be conscious of any media intake and try to listen to voices and music that make us feel great.

**To free your authentic voice from internal blocks, perform this exercise at least three times this week:**

Go into nature alone and sit with your eyes closed, listening. Connect with your surroundings and all living elements with the following steps:

- Focus on your breath.
- Inhale, exhale. With each exhale, start to release your voice through sound.
- Hum.
- Chant.

◉ Set your soul voice free (speaking, praying, or singing however it wants to come out). Allow your voice to flow out without caring how it sounds. Without anyone around, this voice ripples, raising our vibration and harmonizing with the earth.

◉ Repeat this exercise on different days for at least three days, especially if you are experiencing resistance. Notice how each time your voice manifests differently.

## Wisdom Questions

♥ How can you put your passion path into action?

♥ What is your relationship with your voice?

♥ What insights arose from the soul song exercise?

# III
# FINANCIAL FREEDOM

**Affirmation: I draw my personal abundance from an
infinite source.**

*"When you can imagine, you begin to create, and when
you begin to create you realize that you can create a world
that you prefer to live in, rather than a world that you're
suffering in."*

—Ben Okri

*"My mission in life is not merely to survive, but to thrive;
and to do so with some passion, some compassion, some
humor, and some style. If you don't like something, change
it. If you can't change it, change your attitude."*

—Maya Angelou

∞

*12/13/2019 Playa Chiquita, Costa Rica*

*I was awake at 12:12 a.m., and the next afternoon praying.
We wanderlusted after the full moonrise as it lit up the
waters;*

*there was bioluminescence in the breaking waves,
fireflies hovering at the tops of the trees,
orgasming with the touch of the water,
the wind over my bare skin.*

*I feel all the stars align around the constellations—*
*the last full moon of the decade.*
*We are so blessed.*
*I can't seem to slow down for long, only a day of wellness and*
*my fire returns*
*feeling everything at once,*
*sometimes a wave of anxiety that turns to excitement, and*
*we ask ourselves, how did we get here?*

∞

Abundance is a mindset. If we believe in infinite abundance, then we attract it. When I was twenty years old, I wanted to be financially free, able to do anything I wished by the time I was thirty.

I used to think that abundance was just material wealth and numbers in a bank account. Now I recognize that abundance is really about having time to pursue your passions; abundance is food growing in your garden, and true love for self and all beings.

Financial freedom is so rare in our times because most people and families in the world live paycheck to paycheck. In 2020, 53 percent of Americans didn't have an emergency fund, and 49 percent were living paycheck to paycheck.[26]

---

26 Newsroom, "FNBO Releases Data from 2020 'Financial Planning' Survey," fnbo (First National Bank of Omaha, February 19, 2020), https://www.fnbo.com/insights/2020/newsroom/fnbo-releases-2020-financial-planning-survey/.

Because of the way our social and economic systems work, everything has a cost. Most of the population exists in unconscious consumerism, and we are taught to go into debt to purchase things to make us happy. Most of us live outside of our means (we spend more than we earn). This system oppresses people by creating a lifetime of debt and channeling everyone's time into jobs that are not fulfilling—for the individual or the planet.

This issue is especially evident in student loans. For example, "roughly 70 percent of students in the US end up taking out loans to go to college. The average graduate leaves school with around $30,000 in debt. All told, some 45 million US citizens owe $1.6 trillion in student loans—and counting."[27] College debt accrues interest, and many students are paying this loan for life. A large reason I achieved financial freedom was that I came out of university debt-free. This process of turning students into workers is not meant to benefit us, but rather to benefit the capitalist system and stimulate the economy.

## FINANCIAL FREEDOM 101

After working in finance for the first eight years of my career, in my last job, I taught "Finance 101" to store managers and presidents, helping them to become financially savvy. The biggest piece of wisdom I took away from the experience is this:

---

27 Samantha Fields, "70% Of College Students Graduate with Debt. How Did We Get Here?," Marketplace (Minnesota Public Radio, October 1, 2019), https://www.marketplace.org/2019/09/30/70-of-college-students-graduate-with-debt-how-did-we-get-here/.

*Live more simply. Do not spend beyond what you earn on a monthly basis.* In other words, spend less on your lifestyle than you generate in income.

Here are some of the key takeaways from my career in finance and my own personal development as a financially sovereign being:

## *UNDERSTAND AND OBSERVE WHERE YOU ARE NOW.

We can't achieve financial freedom without knowing our starting point. Do a personal financial audit of yourself: How much debt do you have? How much do you have in savings? How much money do you need to feel safe and comfortable?

## *LOOK AT MONEY AS A FLOW OF ABUNDANCE AND POSITIVITY.

Debt can certainly be disheartening. But keep in mind that money is a great resource, even if it appears to carry a burden now. If you view money or currency negatively, you'll subconsciously sabotage your chances of making and keeping it.

We all deserve financial freedom and sovereignty. To achieve it, we need to view currency as an instrument to accomplish our dreams, fuel our vitality, and assist us to thrive.

## *WRITE DOWN YOUR FINANCIAL GOALS. VISUALIZE!

Consider tying your goal to something emotional and tangible. When I accomplished sovereignty, it was because I tied it to a passionate goal. I was twenty-four and had to move back into my parents' house after college and another relationship breakup. This was when I set a financial goal: to move out of my parents' house as soon as possible.

That strong desire kept me driven to reach my goal throughout my journey. In my second year of working as an accountant, spending very little while living with my parents, I was able to save up enough to make a down payment on a condo in Seattle. This enabled me to move out of my parents' house and start paying toward my house every month instead of paying rent. When I decided to travel, I rented out this home for a year, which gave me passive income as I traveled.

You will not fulfill your goal in a month. However, a year or two could be enough time to create significant progress toward your financial goal. Make sure your goal is tied to a particular number and clearly envision your dreams (exercise at the end of Chapter 2 and this chapter). Accept it or not, you will subconsciously be working toward these objectives without even realizing it. Knowing exactly where you are now and setting goals for where you want to be are keys to achieving financial freedom.

## *MAKE A BUDGET. BECOME AWARE.

A critical step toward sovereignty is bookkeeping. In my early twenties, I utilized a tool called Mint. This app made a difference in helping me keep on budget by following my expenses, which categories I overspent in, how much cash I had in all of my accounts, and how much credit card debt I had.

When you get comfortable with keeping a budget, you naturally won't have to track your expenses as much. In addition, you'll probably stop spending on unnecessary items when you begin to consider each expense as an investment in your body, family, community, or the earth. After tracking my expenses for so many years, now I am just aware of what is necessary to purchase and what is not. I am aware of the dangers of unconscious consumption, and I choose to vote with my money, energy, time, and cryptocurrency.

## SPEND LESS, LIVE SIMPLY, & PLANT TREES.

Buying less stuff can actually help you attract more abundance. When you spend less, two things work in your favor. First, you'll have more money to put aside toward your financial freedom. Second, you'll learn that you actually need a lot less than you think to thrive. This helps you put aside more for later.

Major items I cut out from my life include: nail salons, hairdressers, shopping firsthand (now I trade clothes or purchase secondhand), fitness memberships, and buying things at department stores. Nowadays, I try to make and recreate with the stuff I already have, repurpose, or give away. I also try to purchase locally to support my community. It is so important to exchange resources with your direct community. This local market activation will help the health and wealth of your community to blossom.

Today, I am living much more simply than I did in my past life. I grow all my cooking herbs, greens, vegetables, and carbohydrates—primarily breadfruit, yuca, plantain, sweet potato varieties, and *malanga* (taro).

This year, Alan and I invested in setting up water systems, building compost toilets, and regenerating cow pastures into tropical **agroforestry** models. We are in transition to sovereignty through growing our food supply and gaining access to pristine water sources, whether through our well, rainwater collection systems, or the rivers flowing through our farm.

---

## AGROFORESTRY

"Agroforestry . . . is a holistic agricultural management system that integrates trees, shrubs, and edible perennial plants to provide multiple crops resistant to pests and diseases."

–Craig R. Elevitch and Diane Ragone[28]

---

28 Craig R Elevitch, and Diane Ragone. "Breadfruit Agroforestry Guide: Planning and Implementation of Regenerative Organic Methods." National Tropical Botanical Garden. (Breadfruit Institute of the National Tropical Botanical Garden, Kalaheo, Hawaii and Permanent Agriculture Resources, Holualoa, Hawaii, 2018), https://ntbg.org/wp-content/uploads/2020/02/breadfruit_agroforestry_guide_web_edition.pdf.

Planting trees creates so much abundance, because once the trees start fruiting, you can easefully feed birds, animals, your neighbors, your community, and yourself. Planting trees will help your family and community today and support generations to come.

Something that I have learned through the Jungle Project is that one breadfruit tree can meet a family's carbohydrate needs for many generations.

## TREE OF LIFE: BREADFRUIT

"It's important that we prioritize staple carbohydrates that grow on trees, creating lasting nutrition for communities and carbon in the ground at the same time. Working with farmers to plant breadfruit trees is essential. Breadfruit is a highly nutritious source of complex carbohydrates, fiber, protein, vitamins, and minerals. Breadfruit grows best in the tropics, where there is also the most world hunger.

Breadfruit jungles are the perfect food source for areas hit by natural disasters in tropical nations. After Hurricane Maria hit Puerto Rico, it took weeks for promised aid to reach people in need. During that time, parts of the island survived for weeks living off breadfruit. Breadfruit can be a solution for malnourishment, world hunger, and environmental issues.

For millennia, nutrient-packed breadfruit was a staple for Pacific Islanders.

Until recently, bringing breadfruit crops outside the tropics has been difficult because of scale. The trees reproduce slowly from root suckers, and growing just a hundred trees that way takes several years. But now a technique using tissue culture, or micropropagation, allows thousands of trees to be grown in a single month. Jungle Project is stepping into this new reality

> to bring the benefits of the new breadfruit surplus to world markets, and also protect the rights of farmers and safeguard the health of the environment."
>
> —Paul Zink, Agroforestry Expert, CEO and Gustavo Angelo, COO, Co-founders of Jungle Project[29] & Jungle Foods
> @JungleProjectCR
> @Jungle.Foods

Trees have an exponential positive impact. They offer so many opportunities to benefit everyone and everything: people, the environment, food, oxygen, carbon seques-tration, medicines, building materials, wildlife habitats, and economic tools for farmers!

In the long run, material things do not make us happy. We get used to them quickly, and then the novelty wears off. What does make us happy is financial security in the sense of not having to deal with poverty or hunger. This is exactly why we should secure our food and water sources by planting trees, tending gardens, and developing sus-tainable water systems.

## IT'S ABOUT EXPERIENCES, NOT THINGS

Money is only a part of what really makes us happy, and we're learning more about the psychological limits of money every day. According to a study that analyzed data from over 1.7 million people in 164 countries, there is a

---

29 Jungle Project, www.jungleproject.com.

happiness tipping point: "The more you have, the more you want, the study concluded. These findings speak to a broader issue of money and happiness across cultures."[30]

Our happiness *does* increase when we spend time with friends, partners, or family and enjoy nature and quality time, all with good mental health. Doing good in the world—by giving back, lending support to others, or volunteering for a cause—also makes us happy. A 2016 study from the University of the South shows that "random acts of kindness" for others or for the world can boost your mood. Interestingly, the study found that "helping others can boost your mood more than if you had done something to help yourself. Why? It encourages our body to release dopamine, which gives you what some call a 'helper's high.'"[31] A 2017 survey from the Women's Philanthropy Institute noted that people are happier overall when they give to others and that the more they do or give, the happier they tend to be. It's simply referred to as "the joy of giving."[32]

Life's short. We should enjoy it. It's not about *not* consuming; it's about consuming consciously to meet your

30 Quentin Fottrell, "Psychologists Say They've Found the Exact Amount of Money You Need to Be Happy," MarketWatch (MarketWatch, March 4, 2018), https://www.marketwatch.com/story/this-is-exactly-how-much-money-you-need-to-be-truly-happy-earning-more-wont-help-2018-02-14.

31 Lauren Schumacker, "10 Ways Giving Back Can Benefit Your Mental and Physical Health," Insider (Insider Inc., November 16, 2018), https://www.insider.com/how-giving-back-can-benefit-you-2018-11#you-can-feel-an-immediate-surge-in-happiness-1.

32 The NonProfit Times, "Study: People Happier When They Give," The NonProfit Times (Nonprofit Times Publishing Group Inc., October 17, 2017), https://www.thenonprofittimes.com/npt_articles/study-people-happier-give/.

basic necessities and within your means. Ultimately, the things that will help you live a more fulfilled life will be the experiences you have and your inner happiness—not the possessions that you own.

Life is made up of moments. A few experiences will stay with me forever:

*My grandfather would fly my family to visit Maine most Augusts to spend quality time together at camp or his summer cabin beside a lake. I will never forget the time when my brother and I swam over a mile to the other side of the lake. Nor will I forget my entire family hanging out on the screened porch on what we called "Rocking Chair Lane," watching the water.*

*Each summer, my friends and family would go backpacking in the wilderness. We repeated this journey each year up until I moved countries. Our last walk in the mountains was near Lake Ann in Esmeralda Basin, an hour from Seattle. I watched the sun go down before the Perseid meteor shower, filled with gratitude. I couldn't keep track of the shooting stars we saw, there were so many. It was magical to catch one of the biggest meteor showers in the last twenty years. I will treasure these experiences with my brother and family friends forever.*

*On my thirtieth birthday in El Paredon, when I was living off the grid for a few months, Alan took me on a boat ride down a mangrove-lined river and a horse ride along the beach. This was the most romantic gift I could have imagined.*

All these moments make up a lifetime of magical experiences. I think when we can get creative and invite our friends to go for a hike, practice music, go surfing, or share a meal together, these experiences become the memories that stay with us. We can't purchase memories from a store; in all likelihood, we can't purchase them at all. Life is about the moments spent laughing together and sharing adventures with the ones we love.

## TAKE CONTROL OF YOUR ABUNDANCE

We have the ability to create our abundance by taking concrete actions and living our passions. These are a few of the steps I suggest for taking back control:

### *PAY OFF DEBT.

Taking control of your abundance starts with being debt-free. Paying off debt isn't as exciting as having cash in the bank, but it does bring you closer to freedom. It can lift a massive weight off your shoulders. After paying off your debt, you will see the amount of money you have in the bank rise. It's an incredible feeling watching the number climb (even if you had to watch it fall at the beginning), and in my experience, it keeps you motivated to continue growing it.

Not all debt is created equal. Debt from purchasing your home is different from student loans or credit card debt. Why? When you sell your home, most likely your home hasn't depreciated in value (although in some financial cycles this could occur). For instance, I purchased a home in the midst of the economic recession and sold a home eight years later in a booming economy. Most of my friends who are financially free have invested in real estate and land projects, selling their land or properties as their lives change and reinvesting the profits wisely. This ebb and flow of investing, making returns, and reinvesting your money is all part of the journey toward financial freedom.

## *BE A BUSINESS OWNER.

Work for yourself. Offer consulting to others, and create your own schedule. Launch your own project, or partner with others to create your own business or cooperative. By being a business owner or involved in a cooperative, I am building up financial equity through my work. I choose to receive equity in my projects instead of paying myself.

There are tax benefits to being a business owner and holding equity in a project instead of paying yourself out and getting taxed on it.

## *DIVERSIFY YOUR INCOME STREAMS.

If you're serious about financial freedom, you have to start creating new sources of income. It is important to have multiple income streams. The more diversity you have in your income, the less fragile your freedom will be.

If you work for a company in a nine-to-five job, trading your time for money, you're limited by the hours in the day. On the other hand, if you find gig-style work or consult for others, you can control your hours.

There is a multitude of ways to diversify your active income streams:

- Develop your personal brand and monetize your website.

- Become a virtual partner on websites like Upwork, Fiverr, Freelancer, Guru, PeoplePerHour, or Hubstaff Talent.

- Become an independent author, finding occupations on websites like ProBlogger.

- Join gig apps like Lyft, Uber, Grubhub, TaskRabbit, Dumpling, or EasyShift.

- Create a childcare service or elective school service.

- Create an at-home cooking and conveyance service.

- Sell high-quality items at your nearby farmer's market.

- Get work from listings on Craigslist.

- Create online workshops.

- Teach English online.

- Start planting the seeds from the fruit you eat, and sell the saplings or exchange plants with your community.

It's all about time. If you are lacking the time to diversify your earnings through active income, passive income streams allow income to flow in without as much energy invested:

- Sell your junk or secondhand clothing on Shopify, Etsy, or eBay.

- Sell content (blogs, ebooks, books, classes, webinars, audiobooks, or podcasts).

- Become an affiliate marketer for other people's content.

- Buy a real estate investment and lease it out. Or rent out a room in your current home, or create an experience on Airbnb.

- Invest in cryptocurrency.

There are many creative ways to create multiple streams of income. I have been successful in creating passive income through rental income and investing in cryptocurrency. I made my Seattle condo an Airbnb. I would rent it out during the high season and when I traveled out of town for work. With cryptocurrency, I have invested only amounts that I am willing to lose. Over the course of the last few years, I have been able to **dollar-cost average** into buying Bitcoin and other cryptocurrencies successfully. My brother, Brett Pullen, would say, "It's a financial crime to not own Bitcoin in 2021."

---

## DOLLAR-COST AVERAGING

An investment strategy to purchase small sums of an asset over long periods of time to reduce the impact of volatility on the total amount invested.

---

## *INVEST IN YOUR FUTURE. CONTINUE DREAMING AND REEVALUATING YOUR GOALS.

Save for your emergency "rainy day fund" every month. If you set aside money for rainy days in the future, you'll be less likely to end up back where you are now: wishing for financial freedom.

It is also *so* important to reevaluate your financial situation and check in with your heart every so often. For example, when you know you need to sell, get your strategy in place to exit your investment. At my botanical garden beach house in Costa Rica, I watched the surrounding neighborhood grow in popularity. With this growth came more noise, and my peace left. My heart and intuition told me to exit this property investment and sell the house.

It is part of life to make changes, move, and have different desires. As you continue to dream and move through different cycles of your life, be sure to reassess your goals—and always keep acting on them.

## DIVERSITY

Diversity is key in all aspects of life. Diversity on professional teams can mean hiring a range of people of various races, ethnicities, socioeconomic backgrounds, cultures, genders, sexual identities, lifestyles, experiences, or interests. Diversity in agriculture describes a **polyculture** of crops (many different crops) and plenty of biodiversity, which mimics natural forests. Financial diversity, or "diversification," means we have different assets and monetary resources in different asset categories such as cash, stocks, gold, equity, land, cryptocurrencies, and investments in companies.

We have all heard the saying, "Don't put all your eggs in one basket." Well, we can look at finances similarly.

"Uniformity is not nature's way; diversity is nature's way.

In nature's economy the currency is not money,
it is life."

—Vandana Shiva

We must diversify and invest in our earth and the well-being of all our communities:

- ⊚ **Land.** I highly recommend investing in real estate and learning about small-scale farming. True financial freedom comes from living rent-free and growing at least some of your own food. You could get there by owning your own land, or you could live on someone else's land in exchange for helping with the crops. Another option could be building on a friend or family member's land.

  I acknowledge that land ownership is not an ideal system, as there is so much resource inequality around the world. I much prefer certain indigenous philosophies that regard the land as a communal resource, with ownership vested in the group rather than in any one individual.

  We give the greatest gift of abundance to the earth and future generations when we steward our lands, planting organic crops and fruit trees. As we plant and regenerate the land, we increase our shared biological, spiritual, and emotional capital. My partner and I are filled with happiness knowing we are sovereign.

◉ **Water.** Water is life, and it is important to invest in your own natural spring or water source for your community. For example, you can invest in building your own rainwater collection system or creating a well. Water should not be monetized or privatized.

◉ **Regenerative Startups and Community Projects.** When I was looking at mutual funds and green investment vehicles, I was shocked to find that presumably green companies were really just "washed green" with their philanthropic giving. I highly recommend investing in what you oversee. For example, I have invested in aligned initiatives such as Jungle Project and other women-led organizations. I have also invested in my family's farm project in our backyard. Land capital and stewardship can be far more fulfilling than just a monetary investment.

◉ **Cryptocurrency.** The idea of cryptocurrency is to decentralize the banking system and put economic power into the people's hands. I personally recommend purchasing Bitcoin and a few other cryptocurrencies you like, because the future should not be controlled by a select few individuals in charge of the entire global monetary system. And remember, never invest more than you would feel comfortable losing!

☺ **Self-Love.** Each cycle, it is crucial to invest in yourself. If you are your best self, comfortable in your own skin, and full of gratitude for life and joy in the small moments, then you will attract more of that. Like attracts like. Each year, I take at least one retreat or vacation to honor my own needs (yes, this is a privilege). In 2020, I attended the Mujeres Fuertes self-defense experience with Toby Israel; a virtual Aphrodite goddess temple with Camille Willemain; a Mindful Magic Women's Circle with Ciara Lemony; a fermentation class with Lala Palmieri from Weaving Remedies; and a regenerative living class with Sarah Wu at Punta Mona. Invest in yourself; it will come back to you tenfold.

## TIME MANAGEMENT

Before I valued my time like I do now, my schedule was booked up with meetings all day. Sometimes I would even accept meeting requests from different time zones and take calls late in the evening. Many of those meetings seemed to last forever, with no real purpose or goal. I would work weekends to make deadlines for clients.

One day, during my last year in the corporate world, I flipped the switch and took back control of my career and my time. I blocked out full days on the calendar, as well as all mornings and nights, to avoid unexpected meetings and focus on completing meaningful tasks. I also blocked out my lunches and exercise breaks to support my well-being and happiness.

Now, with a different perspective on time, I only schedule recurring virtual meetings for two days of the week. I try to get all my office work done in short and effective working sessions. I minimize my time reading the news or surfing social media. I even shut off my phone at least one day per week. I don't want to live in a virtual world, zooming from meeting to meeting every single day. I need to live in the real and tangible world.

Each week, I also dedicate a day to processing food and creating prepared dishes for the next week, such as root soup, sauces, elixirs, and spreads. A few years ago, I realized that the most expensive products I was buying I could easily make at home. I feel so empowered by fermenting my own homemade kombucha, ginger beer, sauerkraut, and vinegars (recipes in Chapter 7 and online). The medicines I make elevate me. Creating my own medicines at home saves me from purchasing products with uncertain origins or ingredients.

As I think about financial freedom, I realize that time is a large part of it. We live with fullness and freedom when we cut out activities that are not healthy, set boundaries around work or social commitments, and cultivate discipline with movement and exercise.

## CONCLUSION: FINANCIAL FREEDOM

Alan and I are blessed to be sovereign and financially free. We are fortunate to drink fresh, pure water and harvest our meals from the garden. I believe that financial freedom is a critical step toward living fully. Financial freedom can help you take ownership of your finances—and more importantly, your life. The first step of financial freedom is setting your goals and progressing toward them every day!

When we can live with a perspective of abundance instead of scarcity, our life changes for the better. We attract more abundance. It all comes down to consuming within your means, living simply, and making sure that money is consciously spent on your basic needs.

**What are our basic needs? For all of us, these include:**

- Clean Water
- Healthy Food
- Shelter
- Clothing (Secondhand or Local)
- Education
- Electricity
- Love and Connection
- Spirituality

Consuming consciously and living simply allows us to form a symbiotic relationship with nature. Diversifying our investments, our crops, and our trades helps us weather times of crisis such as storms or recessions. As we steward the land, planting and regenerating it, we increase our biological, spiritual, emotional, and cultural capital.

Financial freedom is about our time, too. As soon as we value our own time, we value ourselves, and others value us too. Time is our most precious gift, our most valuable resource. How do you want to spend it?

"You must gain control over your money or the lack of it will forever control you."

—Dave Ramsey

# Guided Inquiry

## Introduction written by Danielle Ashé, Multidimensional High Priestess

"It seemed to me as if most people were living life completely backward, that they were doing so much to get things that they thought would bring them what they desired, but all of this was actually taking them further from  the deeper feeling they were seeking; many had sold their souls and had grown disconnected from their true nature, which led to a greater sense of division, less connection, and a more competitive nature, which made it so much easier for the powers that be to divide and conquer.

Living in such abundance with a small amount of money was liberating; it opened my eyes and heart to the reality that money really doesn't make you happy, although it can be used as a helpful tool.

I received a message from my ancestors speaking loud and clear:

"We see you, we are celebrating you, we are rejoicing; you have finally broken free and you have come so far, for all of us."

We are the change, we are the future, and we're strong on our own, but far stronger together.

This journey has been about returning to nature to re-member our true nature; it's mostly been about finding the courage and aware ness to allow my heart to continue to lead the way to remembrance, which is what my soul came here on Earth to experience.

Sometimes we must forget in order to remember who and what we really are—Love.

And once this is remembered, we mustn't let anything or anyone keep us from living in love and liberation, to truly be the love that we want to see in the world."

# Financial Goal-Setting

"A good financial plan is a road map that shows us exactly how the choices we make today will affect our future."

—Alexa Von Tobel

Assess where you are at with income and debt. Write down your financial goals in a journal, assessing your current situation and creating a budget for your month and year.

Write: *"I will be financially free." "My financial goal is XYZ."* Put this goal into writing and post it somewhere that you will see every day. The more you read and remind yourself of your financial goal, the more you will subconsciously and consciously work toward financial freedom.

## ABUNDANCE MEDITATION

If you would like to dive into an abundance mindset, I highly recommend Deepak Chopra's twenty-one-day abundance meditation course. I listened to it for the first time when the COVID-19 pandemic started, and it helped me to stay positive and focused on abundance. In the months that followed, I experienced more abundance than I ever expected through non-traditional methods—harvests from the farm, exchanges, financial gifts, and full food and water sovereignty at home.

The free course can help you shift your perspective, transcend your limiting beliefs, and develop an abundance mindset.[33]

## Wisdom Questions

- ♥ Am I noticing a perspective of scarcity or abundance in my day-to-day thoughts?

- ♥ In what ways am I experiencing abundance right now?

- ♥ Are my ways of creating income aligned with my passions?

- ♥ Do I have time to follow my heart?

---

33 Chopra 21-Day Meditation Experience (Chopra, 2021), https://chopracentermeditation.com/.

# IV
# PURIFICATION

**Affirmation: I am whole. I am in vibrant health. With each breath comes a new opportunity. I choose to make today a great day.**

*"The wound is the place where the light enters you."*

—Rumi

*"Going inward. That's the real work. The solutions are not outside of us. Get to know who you really are, because as you search for the hero within, you inevitably become one."*

—Emma Tiebens

*"Destroy the idea that you have to be constantly working or grinding in order to be successful. Embrace the concept that rest, recovery, and reflection are essential parts of the progress toward a successful and ultimately happy life."*

—Dan Regan

When I was working from nine to five and traveling most of my career, I was on the go all the time. I set my alarm for early in the morning to exercise and prepare a smoothie and lunch before work. I engaged in networking events, continued my education with ongoing training or workshops, volunteered on the board of a nonprofit, and socialized at happy hours.

Looking back, I feel like I filled up my schedule so much that I had little time left to just *be*, relax, and restore. When the weekend came around, I still had so much personal work to do, just keeping up with laundry, cleaning the house, and doing all the other chores involved in running a household, as I was living alone.

These days, I wake up naturally, without the sound of a phone or alarm jolting my body out of sleep. Instead, the birds and the howler monkeys wake me as the jungle turns from night into day. I take rest throughout the day, and I still have so much time for everything. It helps that I work for myself, and that I drive out of my house only a few times a week.

I have much more time in my day now, especially since I wake with the tropical sun. I typically start my morning with meditation, a big glass of citrus water, a grounding practice, exercise, and a green goddess smoothie. When it is cool in the morning, I enjoy spending time in nature and gardening; when it's hot in the middle of the day, I'm in the shade preparing food or working on regenerative projects. At sunset, Alan and I usually move to the front porch to watch the sun go down, bringing out our instruments and singing songs together.

I like to think of life as a journey where we need to take water breaks, rest regularly, and keep going step by step. When we feel that our body is out of balance, with a headache or upset stomach, or a sense of burnout or fatigue, the best thing we can do is rest immediately, tend to our needs, and maybe serve ourselves a cup of nourishing tea. Remember what flight attendants say on a plane: in the case of an emergency, put on your own oxygen mask first before assisting others.

There are many ways to continually purify our bodies, our physical vessels, throughout our day—and throughout our lifetimes. A few ways that have greatly impacted my life are:

- Meditation
- Fasting
- Plant-Based Eating
- Yoga or Movement
- Time in Nature
- Breathwork

These are the practices that help me keep my literal and metaphorical oxygen levels high, ready for any challenge I may face.

## MEDITATION, SILENCE, & PRESENCE

Meditation came to me after I dismantled my former life. It was a key part of my healing journey and continues to be part of my daily routine. I wish that meditation were taught in every school to children, but I'm grateful to have found it as an adult. I came to meditation through my yoga practice, where I especially loved *savasana* (final resting pose) and the guided meditations that my teachers led.

After that, I started to meditate each morning for a few minutes, first using a guided meditation application, and then practicing longer meditations on my own. I realized that living in the present was the single greatest gift I could give myself.

When I live in the now, my life becomes a ceremony.

"Accept—then act. Whatever the present moment contains, accept it as if you had chosen it. Always work with it, not against it. Make it your friend and ally, not your enemy. This will miraculously transform your whole life."

—Eckhart Tolle, *The Power of Now: A Guide to Spiritual Enlightenment*

Meditation (along with practicing silence) accelerates our awareness of the subtle layers of our being. At times, it can bring deeply buried issues to the forefront of our mind for resolution; at others, it can provide instant access to a state of pure bliss. The continued practice of meditation will calm your mental activity and allow you to become an observer in your own mind. As your meditation practice matures, that sense of inner serenity and balance makes its way into all corners of your life, and you will feel like the happy, steady person you are, inside and out. When we overcome the tyranny of our mind, we free ourselves from the limitations of our mental conditioning.

The mastery of meditation can only be achieved through practice. Luckily, more and more people seem to be jumping on board. According to a study from the Centers for Disease Control and Prevention, 14.2 percent of US adults surveyed in 2017 said they had practiced meditation at least once in the last year.[34] Evidence suggests that meditation can help to improve anxiety levels 60 percent of the time; after meditating for six to nine months, almost two-thirds of those prone to anxiety managed to reduce their anxiety levels.[35]

The biggest distractions from the present moment come from our minds and from our phones, computers, and other digital technologies. Sometimes we forget about the real world in front of us because we are so absorbed in the virtual world. I remember being single and sitting down next to a man at the airport who was using Tinder on his phone, swiping away, when I was single and sitting right next to him. He didn't even look up. I smiled and laughed to myself about how virtual our world has become.

---

34 Eliza Barclay and Julia Belluz, "The Growth of Yoga and Meditation in the US Since 2012 Is Remarkable," Vox (Vox Media, LLC, January 3, 2019), https://www.vox.com/2018/11/8/18073422/yoga-meditation-apps-health-anxiety-cdc.

35 Jason Ong and David Sholtes, "A Mindfulness-Based Approach to the Treatment of Insomnia," *Journal of Clinical Psychology* 66, no. 11 (2010): pp. 1175-1184, https://doi.org/10.1002/jclp.20736.

Technology can be a weapon that kills us halfway, or we can use it as a tool for our creations. Balance is everything. I didn't have a smartphone until I was twenty-three. Today, young kids are on devices all the time, the virtual world shaping their minds. The constant bombardment of notifications from people, advertising, and information sources often creates unnecessary noise. People of all ages are losing their connection to nature—and their own inner nature.

The first time I realized I was addicted to my phone, and that my head was tired from all the noise, was in Vipassana.

---

## VIPASSANA

Vipassana is one of India's most ancient meditation techniques. Vipassana means seeing things as they really are.[36]

---

In 2016, my solo travels brought me to a Vipassana meditation center in Washington state. Of all the profound experiences in my life, this one changed me the most, helping me purify my being and come back to myself and nature. **Vipassana Meditation** is a process of self-purification by self-observation. Typically, a Vipassana experience consists of a ten-day silent meditation course in

---

36 "Vipassana," Vipassana Meditation (Dhamma.org), accessed November 2, 2021, https://www.dhamma.org/en/about/code.

nature, where participants learn to observe the natural breath to concentrate the mind.

With a sharpened awareness, meditators often proceed to observe the changing nature of the body and mind, experiencing the universal truths of impermanence, suffering, and egolessness. Realizing these truths through experience is a process of purification.

∞

### 9/14/2016 Vipassana Center, Mount Saint Helens, Washington State

#### Day 1: Pain, Fear, Wanting to Escape

*During my teacher-student appointment, I tell my teacher how uncomfortable I feel, "like I want to escape my own body." The videos of discourses and teachings confirm my feelings: we all have knots and barriers. In order to understand the universe, we need to break down our own knots.*

#### Day 2: Self-Forgiveness, Grace, Threads of Light

*I sleep through the first 4:30 a.m. meditation hour; I guess my body is telling me I need to rest to be able to learn and get through the day. I don't feel as much pain as I meditate, and I am able to focus on my breath. It's interesting how cravings do go away. Hunger, tiredness, and pain are all mental.*

### Day 3: Slowing Down, Calming

*My mind is more aware. I only have a few moments of extreme discomfort.*

### Day 4: The Beginning

*The morning is magical with the dew on the grass and the sunrise over the mountains. Everything slows down even more as I listen to the deer breathe.*

*Today we learn to body-scan in meditation and feel every sensation. The mind needs to be retaught and reprogrammed to change.*

### Day 5: Awakening

*We normally do very little to observe all the natural sensations of our own bodies. There is so much to explore just by scanning my body from head to toe. I notice and feel more than I have ever experienced. Tears fall down my cheeks as I feel twitches, heat, or itching—all of which pass or change all the time. I feel blood pulsing through my veins, my breath on my lips, my exposed skin turning to goosebumps in the breeze.*

*I feel my heart opening, my emotions heightening, and my mind changing. I have a moment where my entire body is buzzing, almost like I am spinning.*

*Each time I meditate I feel different; my mind and body are changing. I can never expect the same. I feel like some past pain has come up along the path of sitting with myself for so many days and scanning my body.*

*Here is what I discover:*
◉ *I have male trust issues due to being raped by a colleague in university.*
◉ *I have fear around my mother dying and being left alone without her. Left behind.*

### Days 6 and 7: Ecstasy

*I experience an entire day of ecstasy. I feel high each time I meditate, like my body is buzzing from head to toe, toe to head. By evening, I'm on a six-hour high. It crashes by the last meditation of the day, and I'm craving the feeling again.*

*I feel like I have completed my Vipassana experience, and I almost leave the course three days early. I go out to stargaze and see a meteor shower.*
*I feel like I am in heaven on earth. I am.*

∞

Through the experience of Vipassana, I was able to sit with my deepest darkness, feel my pain deeply throughout my body, and finally release my own need for control, acknowledge my fears, and come to be at peace with all—just the way it is. Each time we sit with ourselves, it is a special ritual, a time to be with ourselves in silence. I often like to end my meditation in prayers or a moment of gratitude.

## GRATITUDE

At least once a day, my family shares gratitude with those around us. We share gratitude before each meal in appreciation for the food that is our medicine and the center of our day. If you're new to the practice of gratitude, you may like to start with a gratitude journal.

Meditation is a tool that I use every day. I now think of it as a routine, like brushing my teeth. It helps me slow down and set intentions before I start my day. With meditation, I set my entire day up with a clear mind and open heart. There are many forms of meditation—movement, yoga, singing, deep breathing, mindfulness—so you can absolutely find something that works for you. I highly recommend adopting some form of meditation as a daily practice. Practicing meditation can increase your attention span after only four days, and it can increase your productivity by 120 percent, so you'll probably notice a difference very quickly.[37]

Meditation in general, and Vipassana specifically, has helped me in every aspect of my life. I came to understand that my greatest limiting factor was my own mind. I also learned that storms don't last forever. A sense of peace and tranquility always follows. That is the beauty of impermanence.

---

37 Eliza Barclay and Julia Belluz, "The Growth of Yoga and Meditation in the US since 2012 Is Remarkable," Vox (Vox Media, LLC, January 3, 2019), https://www.vox.com/2018/11/8/18073422/yoga-meditation-apps-health-anxiety-cdc.

"Mindfulness is a miracle by which we master and
restore ourselves."

—Thich Nhat Hanh

## FAMILY CONSTELLATIONS

After my Vipassana experience, I could feel the inner
healing work that I had done. I recognized patterns I had
never spoken of before. In the months that followed, I
learned about the concept of cosmic family and **family
constellations**. I discovered that we all have patterns in
our families and ancestral lines, and that each family and
culture is different, but also similar. Different degrees of
trauma, violence, war, and darkness exist in every lineage.

---

### FAMILY CONSTELLATIONS

Family constellations attempt to reveal unacknowledged dynamics
that span multiple generations in a given family. They can help to
resolve the deleterious effects of those dynamics by encouraging the
subject, through symbolic representatives of various family members,
to confront and accept their past.

---

After Vipassana, I broke my silence about being raped by
a "friend" in college and shared the story with my mother. My mother was raped in her early twenties by a boy-
friend, and she never told anyone until after I told her my
own story. I was raped in my early twenties and it took
me eight years to tell my mother due to feelings of shame

and guilt. I felt like it must have been partly my fault for putting myself in the situation.

As we recognize patterns and speak out about them, we release our suffering or shame, and the energy transforms. Then we find that we are empowering others to be vulnerable and speak out about their family patterns or personal histories, too.

We have to talk about our traumas. Each time we can transform energy from fear into love, let go of control, and forgive ourselves, we become lighter. Life is a constant healing process, a continual shedding of skins as we grow and evolve, peeling back another layer of the self. As we transform, our capacity to love becomes even greater.

We can choose to break our ancestral legacies of attachment and suffering. We must do so, because when we don't heal these traumas, they can surface as internal illnesses such as cancer or depression, limiting our capacity to thrive.

## REWILDING

"My bones, heart, intention, skin, and more . . . all serving the purpose of my creation. Lately, I'm clearing the old deeper and deeper . . . . flowing into the new. To be honest, it hasn't always been a flow. At times, it was crashing waves of uncertainty and fear. But the Magic is found in continuing forward beyond those resistances.

Choosing MYSELF, over and over. This has become my strongest weapon of discernment. Always choosing myself, with love and Grace. Letting go of loads that feel too heavy. Choosing the way that brings a smile each time.

I AM wild, indigenous Power. Held and free.

My magic is captured in every moment."

–Estonia Kersey Otieno, Earth Healer, Community Leader,
Entrepreneur
@JungleMoonMama

When I am inhabiting the best version of me, or my highest self, I feel like the artist of every moment, painting brushstrokes of joy and breathing in sweetness. When I am in the darkness of struggle and suffering, feeling everything all at once, I try to enjoy the *feeling* of feeling, and I allow myself to feel and weep. It is important for me to radically release emotions as they come. If I don't, these emotions can get stuck in my body in different ways, such as pain in my shoulders or various dis-eases and discomforts.

## FASTING

Fasting is a reset that purifies the body from the inside out, giving our digestive system a vacation to regenerate and clean. My brother and I first learned about fasting when we were looking into natural cures to cancer for our mom. A full-body cleanse is commonly suggested for anyone concerned about their physical, emotional, mental, and spiritual well-being.

"A coconut water fast will repair and remineralize all the tissues in your body. It will provide your body with nutrients and hydration on a cellular level, while simultaneously triggering a detoxification response. Pipa water is the biggest source of electrolytes (positively charged minerals) in the world and will begin to electrically charge and cleanse the body simultaneously as it matches the plasma of the blood (55 percent of the blood). Try to drink 10 to 20 coconuts per day for 5 days."

—Dr. Gregory Damato, PhD, Founder,
The SuperHero Program[38]

∞

### 12/18/2018 El Paredon, Guatemala

*We have been drinking lots of coconuts and eating lots of fruit.*
*Fasting on cocos.*
*Cacao ceremony.*
*Washed by the ocean.*
*Singing to the stars.*
*Warmed by the fire.*
*Honeymooning with ourselves.*
*Surfing.*

---

38 "The Superhero Program," The SuperHero Program, accessed November 2, 2021, http://www.thesuperheroprogram.com/.

*Feeling clearer.*
*Regenerated. Mind. Body. Spirit. Child.*
*Lover of life. Gracias Mama. Mama Earth. Pachamama.*
*For all the divine feminine. Sisters.*
*Brothers. Mothers. Fathers. Abuelos. Abuelitas.*
*Seed.*
*Plant.*
*Grow.*
*Expand.*

∞

Based on my experience, I highly recommend an annual five-day coconut fast. Coconuts are the purest form of hydration! If you are not in the tropics, an organic juice fast or the Master Cleanse[39] are nice options to look into. With coconuts, juice, or the Master Cleanse, you will be able to keep up high energy levels—as opposed to the draining effects of plain water fasting. It is always recommendable to rest and relax plenty during fasting periods.

∞

### 8/4/2017 Seattle, Washington, Master Cleanse

*Just like in meditation, when I observe a thought come into my mind or a pain in my body, I observe waves of hunger. Everything is impermanent and eventually passes. The Master*

---

39 "How to Do the Master Cleanse," Maple Valley Cooperative, August 11, 2021, https://maplevalleysyrup.coop/how-to-do-the-master-cleanse-lemonade-diet/.

*Cleanse is a beautiful and painful experience that consists of only consuming lemonade with maple syrup and cayenne pepper (typically for ten days, but I did mine for five). Just like with meditation, the battle is physiological at first, but then come peace and clarity.*

*For me, the first day was filled with doubt, and time passed so slowly—hunger, pain, and fatigue. By the third day, the hunger subsided, and I was energized.*

*Food is life. After not eating for five days, I have a great appreciation and love for food. My connection to this sacred relationship with food excites me to prepare, ferment, grow, and experiment.*

∞

## THE BODY IS A TEMPLE

As an environmentalist and an animal lover, I choose to eat a variety of plant-based, whole, organic, regenerative foods grown in my garden or purchased from local farmers and markets. (I just dropped so many labels there, it was like a rap song!) My body and mind are happiest without meat or dairy. I have experimented on myself for over seven years, exploring different diet choices such as fully organic, partly regenerative, vegan, vegetarian, and raw. My body feels nourished. I prefer not to label myself by any specific diet; I trust my inner knowing to decide what my needs are in different cycles.

We all have intuitive knowledge about what makes us feel most vibrant and alive. It is so important to trust our intuition on what our body needs and also be conscious of our consumption at the same time. The documentary *Forks Over Knives* drastically influenced my lifestyle and diet. It talks about *The China Study*, which found that people who consume fewer animal products—only eating meat as a condiment for their rice and vegetables—live longer and with fewer illnesses. In *The China Study*, Dr. T. Colin Campbell "details the connection between nutrition and heart disease, diabetes, and cancer."[40]

When I moved to Costa Rica in 2017, I learned about **Blue Zones,** where people commonly live past the age of one hundred. The Nicoya Peninsula in Costa Rica has been named one of the top five Blue Zones in the world; on average, residents there live even longer than those in the rest of the country.[41] The conventional diet in the Nicoya Peninsula is comprised of rice, beans, and homemade corn tortillas with homegrown crops such as bananas, plantains, papaya, squash, *pejibaye* (palm fruit), yams, and black beans.

---

40 Thomas Campbell, *The China Study: the Most Comprehensive Study of Nutrition Ever Conducted and Startling Implications for Diet, Weight Loss, and Long-Term Health* (Benbella Books, 2017).

41 "Nicoya, Costa Rica," Blue Zones, May 4, 2021, https://www.bluezones.com/exploration/nicoya-costa-rica/.

## BLUE ZONES

Blue Zone is a term coined by Dan Buettner in reference to five areas of the world where an uncommonly high percentage of the population lives to be one hundred or older. People living in Blue Zones tend to be happier and healthier, exercising more, living off the land, and eating a mostly plant-based diet.

"The calculus of aging offers us two options: We can live a shorter life with more years of disability, or we can live the longest possible life with the fewest bad years. As my centenarian friends showed me, the choice is largely up to us."

—Dan Buettner, *The Blue Zones Kitchen: 100 Recipes To Live To 100*

When my mom was first diagnosed with ovarian cancer, my brother hopped on a vegan diet, and my dad, mom, and I all went almost completely plant-based. My mom's illness illuminated for us how important it is to feed our bodies with the highest-energy, most alive ingredients. As I learned in *Forks Over Knives,* "Even when processed foods and animal products are sold cheaply, they are expensive in terms of the cost to your health." In my transition to plant-based cuisine, I have become more adventurous with the food I cook. Creativity in the kitchen makes my life fun and meaningful.

Plant-based diets are not just better for our bodies; they are better for our environment as well. For example, agriculture is responsible for 80–90 percent of US water consumption, and growing food crops for livestock is responsible for 56 percent of water consumption in the US.[42]

**According to scientific research,[43] the land required to feed one person for one year is as follows:**

- ◉ Vegan: 1/6 acre

- ◉ Vegetarian: 3x as much as a vegan

- ◉ Meat Eater: 18x as much as a vegan

---

## ORGANIC

Until we eat truly organic food, we are still exposing ourselves to agrochemicals. Eating organic also means we are getting more minerals and nutrients from our plants and vegetables. As Maria Rodale writes in her Organic Manifesto, non-organic food is poisoning us:[44]

"We are allowing a few major global corporations in collusion with our government to poison us along with the bugs, the fungi, the weeds, and the increasingly common crop diseases. What is wrong with us? Why do we seem to care so little about our own safety, our own health, and the future of our children? The most important point is that growing scientific evidence suggests that toxic chemicals we are using to grow food are destroying us."

---

42 "The Sustainability Secret," COWSPIRACY (Animals United Movement A.U.M., 2014), https://www.cowspiracy.com/facts.

43 "The Sustainability Secret," COWSPIRACY (Animals United Movement A.U.M., 2014), https://www.cowspiracy.com/facts.

44 Maria Rodale, *Organic Manifesto: How Organic Farming Can Heal Our Planet, Feed the World, and Keep Us Safe* (New York, NY: Rodale, 2011), p. 30.

Just as we purify our minds, we must also purify our temples (the body) and our environment. We cannot purify the body if we continue to expose it to the toxins in our waters, cosmetics, sunscreens, shampoos, and other cleaning products. We need to do a complete overhaul of the products we consume.

If you don't understand the ingredients list, then don't purchase the product. I use coconut oil for everything body- and cooking-related, and vinegar for everything cleaning-related. I stopped wearing makeup, except for using *achiote* seeds (from the lipstick tree!) to color my lips for special occasions. I purchase only biodegradable products for laundry and soaps. I purchase handmade herbal products from Weaving Remedies[45] and other herbal products from local women.

Our body is our temple. What we feed it—pure water, food, information, and other products—is so important, as is the environment we live in. For me, going mostly plant-based is a lifestyle choice and ethic that I strive for. The research on plant-based and organic diets is compelling, but the real shift happened for me when I lived it.

45  https://www.instagram.com/weaving.remedies/.

## WATER

"Gives us the key,
Gives us new life,
Shows us to be,
Water.
Leading the way,
Stronger she grows,
Each time we pray,
Water.
That falls from the sky,
You make rivers for me,
You create streams for me,
Water.
Shows wisdom
From the bottom of the Earth,
Of the depths of your Heart,
Water.
Your language is infinite,
Your language is infinite,
From waves and whirls,
In the tide of the ocean,
Water.
Blesses all of Life,
From the bottom of the Earth,
of the depths of your Heart.

The water of the Earth will heal you.
The water of the Earth will heal you. "

–Ciara Lemony,[46] Healer, Ceremonialist, Artist,
& Musician
@ciaralemony, @jewels.light, @water.of.the.earth

46 Ciara Lemony, https://ciaralemony.com/.

## CONCLUSION: PURIFICATION

Purifying the mind and body and feeding our temple in all ways are important parts of thriving. We mimic our environment. If we are sick, then the earth is too—and vice versa. We need to continually regenerate ourselves by taking care of our environment. We need to continually regenerate ourselves in order to take *better* care of our environment.

Meditation helps us to relax, decrease our stress levels, deal with anxiety, and sleep better. It's not a surprise that this ancient practice is growing in popularity. Meditation roots us in the present moment, supporting our relaxation and our connection to nature. Fasting every year helps to restore our cells, while eating local, whole, plant-based, and organic foods is essential to keeping our life force vibrant and nourished.

As Maria Rodale of the Rodale Institute says in *Organic Manifesto,*

> "Here is what we know: Plants, animals, and people have immune systems. When we are in the natural environment and take good care of ourselves—eat right, exercise, sleep well, use basic hygiene techniques, feel loved and cared for and actively take part in our communities—our immune systems are typically healthy and strong . . . . When we try to sterilize our environment (or the extreme, let it be truly dirty) or try to exterminate a weed, an insect, or a disease,

nature fights back just as we would, launching even stronger attacks. The result is viruses, disease, and superpests that become resilient to pesticides. The more we try to isolate ourselves and control nature the weaker and more vulnerable we become."[47]

It's all about the journey to getting in touch with yourself, your heart, and nature. It is not about immediate change. It's about gently introducing yourself to a lifestyle that is healthier, more sustainable, and interconnected with all beings. It is about transitioning to living with more simplicity and health—for ourselves and the planet.

Each time we surface another layer of our human existence and heal it, it's like peeling back another layer of an onion. The inner work of releasing stories, patterns, and past traumas goes hand in hand with the work of purifying the physical body, our temple. It's important to make our own medicines through our food and establish healthy rituals to connect back to ourselves and the nature around us. When we purify our bodies and minds, we can show up as our best selves for our families, our communities, and our planet.

"Your task is not to seek for love, but merely to seek and find all the barriers within yourself that you have built against it."

—Rumi

---

47 Maria Rodale, in *Organic Manifesto: How Organic Farming Can Heal Our Planet, Feed the World, and Keep Us Safe* (New York, NY: Rodale, 2011), p. 36.

# Guided Inquiry

**Intro written by Ahimsa Ongwenyi,[48] Health Coach,
Remembrance Guide @betheloveyouare**

### Body Temple

"I focus on tending to the health of my body so that it may be the sanctuary for Spirit and the beacon of creative expression that it was always intended to be.

I love supporting and guiding others in tending to their health and embodying their well-being so that they may become their own sanctuary once again as well.

Lately, I'm remembering how naturally this comes to me, and it makes my cells buzz looking back on times that visually reflect these revelations.

I've traveled many places, will travel many more, and have many homes around the world within my heart, yet this will always be my body's home environment.
My body thrives when immersed in these tropical elements. I receive all of the forms of hydration and nourishment that I need. My energy is ridiculously magnetic and I feel crystal clear in my godly essence. My simplest and grandest desires are met with ease.

---

48 www.bethelovethatyourare.org or https://www.youtube.com/betheloveyouare.

In this moment, I am actively calling in more sunshine and papayas, salty air and sandy skin, mountain views and minimal clothes, barefoot days and nights filled with the symphony of the jungle, all the fruits, a peaceful home—every little thing that supports our health, our joy, our mission, and our thriving.

We are all here to thrive, my loves.

Remember it. Say it. Claim it. Embody it. Live it. And eat more fruit!"

# Create a New Habit

Set a time in your daily routine to meditate for the next twenty-one days. Practice meditating for ten minutes each day. Let go of attachment to where your mind is and simply sit with what is present:

1. **Set up your space** to meditate free of distractions.
2. **Set the time.** Dusk or dawn are the most favorable times, but select any time to make it easy for you to adopt a meditation practice for the next twenty-one days.
3. **Make it a habit.** Try to meditate at the same time each day. For me, my meditation time is before I get out of bed.
4. **Find a comfortable seated position.** The psychic current needs to travel unimpeded from the base of the spine to the top of the head. This will help center the mind and encourage concentration. (Another option is to take a silent nature walk each morning or evening.)
5. **Breathe.** Start by observing the breath.
6. **Choose concentration.** Choose to keep listening to the breath and holding your posture. You can scan your body from head to toe to keep your focus.
7. **Notice how you feel** after twenty-one days, and see if you want to adopt this as an ongoing practice in your healthy and happy life.

## STREAM-OF-CONSCIOUSNESS JOURNALING

Start a gratitude journal or journal with the new moon and full moon. Journaling can help us process and release emotions.

Exercise written by Eva Dalak, Coaching, Training, Leadership, and Transformation @evadalak

"When I feel the need to connect or express myself,
I often turn to introspection.
I start this process with two tools—a pen and a piece of paper.
My goal is simple: just write out everything I'm feeling.
It helps me to know there's no time limit on this process
and there's no page length requirement. It's a way for me
to hold space for myself and acknowledge what I'm feeling.
I don't hold back, I let it all out on the paper.
Every single time, I experience a shift."

## Wisdom Questions

♥ How does my heart feel?

♥ What emotions am I processing?

♥ How does my body react to different foods?

♥ How do I feel when I eat food in its purest form and pure spring water?

♥ Do I have any dis-ease that purification practices could help heal?

# V
# SEEDS OF LOVE

**Affirmation: I am love. Love is within me. Love surrounds me.**

*"Let the beauty of what you love be what you do."*

—Rumi

*"Love the life you live.*
*Live the life you love."*

—Bob Marley

On February 11, 2018, Alan and I affirmed our commitment to each other in a love ceremony overlooking an active volcano in Lake Arenal. Sitting in a circle above a jungle food forest, we drank cacao and shared our celebration with a few close friends and family members. Together, we spent the weekend vacationing, savoring different foods and spoiling ourselves with the best varieties of exotic fruits. We woke up before sunrise to lie in a hot river flowing from Mount Arenal; the sun's first rays touched our bodies, and the steam evaporated into the thick, tropical jungle canopy.

This was a completely different way of celebrating than a traditional wedding, but it felt so dear to us. Our commitment to our relationship was also a commitment to our personal growth paths, nourishing the physical and metaphorical garden surrounding us, and planting the seeds of our own paradise. Our love vows were the following:

*When I met you, I had set myself free. When I am with you, I am freer. You empower me to be the best version of myself. I love you for who you are yesterday, today, and tomorrow.*
*Your heart, your spirit.*
*You are a beautiful reflection of love,*
*A servant to this earth protecting animals, plants, and humans.*
*I love you as a child, a grandmother, a father, a brother, a lover, and an animal.*

*I promise to be impeccable with my words.*
*To not take anything personally.*
*To not make assumptions.*
*And to do the best I can.*

*I know that we can travel this journey together in this human existence—through all the waves of life. Supporting each other. Taking time for self-love and care, so that we are able to share this love together. Growing seeds in the ground, in our hearts, and in others.*
*We continue to expand, change, and regenerate.*
*I promise to love you like I love myself. Treating you the way I want to be treated.*
*You are always free with me. To do all your heart desires.*

## FLY (FIRST LOVE YOURSELF)

Until we love ourselves, we are not capable of loving nature or all beings. After the dismantling of one life, it took me a year and a half to come back to self-love and nature. I went through a phase of sadness and darkness, overwhelmed by witnessing human destruction, feeling isolated, and questioning everything. I was mad and frustrated with the status quo. I started to realize that I did not want to follow in the tracks of most of the people around me.

> "Taking care of nature is taking care of humans. Taking care of humans is taking care of nature."
>
> —Kenny Ausubel, Bioneer Co-founder

It was through my purification practices and following my passion that I began to fall in love with each moment, in love with each person, and in love with life itself. I came back to the essence of love: *to know thyself is to love thyself.* Once I entered this state of love, feeling this beautiful energy within and around me, then I attracted a partner who also felt pure, unconditional love for nature, animals, and himself.

Every day, I fall in love with flowers and butterflies and little fungi, talk to the trees, and watch the fish kiss me in the river pools. It is a constant dance of romance with myself as I admire the simple beauty of these details. This feeling of love is universal. Most religions and philosophies describe this feeling of love as God . . . . I believe that God and love are one and the same.

"There are two basic motivating forces: fear and love. When we are afraid, we pull back from life. When we are in love, we open to all that life has to offer with passion, excitement, and acceptance. We need to learn to love ourselves first, in all our glory and our imperfections. If we cannot love ourselves, we cannot fully open to our ability to love others or our potential to create. Evolution and all hopes for a better world rest in the fearlessness and open-hearted vision of people who embrace life."

—John Lennon

## LOVE IS OUR NATURE

The way I see it, love is the highest vibration we can feel. Love is the frequency of the earth, and it exists in everything. Love is a garden that we need to continually nourish with our care and attention—and water. We can look at love the same way we look at a forest; when we see how the flowers, trees, insects, fungi, and fauna all coexist together, we understand that this ecosystem has been perfectly orchestrated to flow. Love is like that.

We humans are complex. Unlike other organisms, we think about the future and the past, and we contemplate the existence of all other beings. We are meant to thrive; we are meant to feel the love at the core of our being.

There is no separation between us and the universe of love that surrounds us and fills us. We are interconnected with all life on this planet, and we are made from stardust.

> "Love is not an intellectual concept or a moral imperative or anything else. It is a background emotion that exists when one is connected to the energy available in the universe, which, of course, is the energy of God . . ."
>
> —James Redfield, *Celestine Prophecy*[49]

As I was traveling through Mexico and Central America, I trusted that each person I met was part of my path, there to teach me certain lessons. I trusted—and continue to trust—my intuition. When the energy of a place or person feels uncomfortable or uncertain, I cross the street, leave the room, or I move away. I believe we can all tap into our gut to know when a situation does not feel good—and when it does.

During my travels, I fell in love with many people, places, towns, homes, forests, and parks. I don't mean sexually; I mean intellectually, cosmically, with appreciation for the differences and unique cultures I saw. I felt like I was meeting the brothers, mothers, grandmothers, and sisters that I needed in each moment. The love I am talking about is a compassionate connection that is free

---

49 James Redfield, *The Celestine Prophecy: An Adventure* (New York, NY: Grand Central Publishing, 2018).

of judgement. It does not come from the mind but rather directly from the heart and soul. Living from love essentially starts with the self. Having love for yourself means that you don't beat yourself up for past mistakes; instead, you learn from the past and keep moving toward unconditional love and acceptance.

> "Bhakti is LOVE—loving God, loving your own self, and loving all beings. The small heart should become bigger and bigger and eventually, totally expansive! A spark can become a forest fire."
>
> —Ammachi, Spiritual Teacher

Love means seeing beauty in every situation—even when it's messy.

∞

### 2/11/2019 Arenal Volcano, Costa Rica

*I love more than I even knew existed.*
*This last year feels like a lifetime of experiences:*
*Waves.*
*Starting with our love ceremony.*
*Envisioning a simple life.*
*In a garden.*
*Noticing the beauty in the simple things.*
*Facing death.*
*The sorrow of missing the woman who birthed me.*
*A phenomenal woman*

*She is.*
*Rising back up.*
*Coming home to paradise.*
*Mama Ocean holding me*
*Sound healing me.*
*Falling back in love with life.*
*Seeing how dark even paradise can be.*

*Women circling together.*
*Sharing and empowering each other through these blocks.*
*Mirrors for each other.*
*Sisters mothers grandmothers.*
*We see patterns repeat.*

*I am free. We are free.*
*Coming back to the garden.*
*Coming back to my seed.*
*Designing systems to become regenerative.*
*We tell each other when we forget to love ourselves.*
*We are strong enough to call each other out.*
*To grow through our mistakes.*
*To see the beauty in the mess.*

∞

Each time I dig deep into the darkness—the bottomless cave of traumas and social illness—I then come back into the light and it shines even brighter. The **Toltec Way** taught me how to make choices that result in love and happiness. This philosophy—or way of life—is based on the key concept that we don't really see life at all; what we actually see is our filter system, which is composed of our beliefs, expectations, agreements, and assumptions.

---

### TOLTEC WAY[50]

The Toltec Way is a path that teaches us to transcend our limiting beliefs and self-sabotaging patterns of behavior in order to live a fulfilling and authentic life. Toltec Way philosophy centers on four agreements:

- ◉ Be impeccable with your word.
- ◉ Don't take anything personally.
- ◉ Don't make assumptions.
- ◉ Always do your best.

---

The more I follow these agreements, the less internal and external drama I experience. I used to want to try to change things about my partners or family, but now I realize that I just love them for where they are. I accept them fully on their own unique life paths. However, that doesn't mean that I don't have boundaries. With family, especially, I set boundaries around hot topics that I know will be triggers. For example, when we're together we try not to talk about politics, capitalism, or dietary choices. I don't want to waste energy on these arguments when I

---

50 Miguel Ruiz and Janet Mills, "The Three Toltec Masteries," The Four Agreements (Amber-Allen Publishing, Inc., April 16, 2020), https://www.thefouragreements. com/the-three-toltec-masteries/.

can simply accept our different perspectives and focus on enjoying their company.

Learning to see past my filters with the Toltec Way, I have recognized that in the moments in my life where I felt like an alien, or different from my peers, I was really just separated from my core self, from love. As I began to explore my passion path and leave behind what was comfortable, I remember my mom saying, "I think we are losing you." She wanted to hold onto our past stories. She wanted me to stay faithful to the image in her head of who I used to be, instead of accepting me in the present. The only constant in life is change. My mom acknowledged my metamorphosis as she was beginning to deteriorate from cancer, and she accepted me with unconditional love.

At the core of all beings is a seed of love. Love grows and flourishes within each of us, especially if we can start our day with intention, appreciation of nature, and conscious consumption. Love can be compared to the "flowering of a plant when the necessary stage of maturity has been reached."[51] We each hold the ability to love—this seed, this potential—within us. It is up to us to nourish this seed of love with compassion, hope, grace, and positive affirmations.

---

51 Michael Soulé, "Love and Its Meaning in the World, a Lecture by Rudolf Steiner, Dec 1912," Lead Together (Lead Together , March 19, 2019), https://leadtogether. org/love-and-its-meaning-in-the-world-a-lecture-by-rudolf-steiner-dec-1912/.

## SEEDS

Seeds represent the foundations or building blocks of life. Just as many of us have lost our connection to ourselves and nature, seeds have been lost too. 93 percent of native and criolla seeds were lost between 1903 and 1993. It is believed that we have lost over 75 percent of Earth's forests due to deforestation and human activity.[52]

"A seed is a forest inside out."
—Matshona Dhliwayo

We depend on trees and seeds for nourishment, for medication, for oxygen—for our survival. In numerous ways, you can follow the underpinnings of any given culture through the legacy of their crops and seeds. Once considered to be available to all, like water, seeds have ended up generally privatized, such that now a few companies presently control the worldwide seed supply.

---

52 Greenpeace, "Forest Destruction," Greenpeace Australia Pacific (Greenpeace), accessed November 2, 2021, https://www.greenpeace.org.au/what-we-do/protecting-forests/forest-destruction/.

## SEEDS

What types of seeds do we have today?

**Local or Native Seeds.** These seeds originate in the land or region where they are currently cultivated. Ten thousand years ago, humans started to domesticate plants and adapt to specific local conditions; their seeds adapted with them.[53]

**Criolla or Adapted Seeds.** These seeds originally come from other regions of the world but have adapted to the climate and soil where they are now grown. With the invasion of colonization, and specifically the Spanish here in Latin America, many seeds have been carried into the Americas–and all across the world.

**Genetically Modified Organism (GMO) Seeds.** These seeds are bred not in a garden but rather in a laboratory, using modern biotechnology techniques like gene splicing. Scientists modify a seed's DNA to ensure that the resulting plant produces desired characteristics. Many GMO seeds are sterile, meaning they cannot produce seeds for the next harvest. Today, three agrochemical giants– Bayer (who bought out Monsanto in 2008), Corteva, and Syngenta– along with a few other large companies control 70 percent of the market. This has drastically reduced biodiversity across the globe.[54]

---

Farming has been around for ten thousand years, but the privatization of seeds has happened in the last one hundred years. Since World War II, "seed diversity has deteriorated, farmers have been put out of business due

---

53 National Geographic Society, "Domestication," (National Geographic Society, October 9, 2012), https://www.nationalgeographic.org/encyclopedia/domestication/.
54 "The Dangerous Concentration of the Seed Market," Public Eye (Public Eye, 2021), https://www.publiceye.ch/en/topics/seeds/concentration-of-the-seed-market.

to rising seed costs, and the pesticide companies control most of the seeds available on the market."[55]

Through the preservation of seeds—planting them on our lands and storing them in seed banks—we can exchange seeds, plant seeds, and bring back some of the biodiversity and vitality we have lost. Seeds are the foundation of all existence. As guardians of the land, we are seeds of change, regeneration, and love. Seeds are our connection to life itself; we cannot have life without seeds.

## LOVE IS A FIRE INSIDE

"Love grows in spaciousness where it can breathe. How often do we choke this flame by following the path of "should," filling ourselves with things that don't actually feed us, listening to outside opinions, saying yes when we mean no, sacrificing ourselves for others who don't want/deserve/require it, judging what we most deeply want, betraying ourselves to be pleasing, and dishonoring the divinity within? How often do we sell our souls for the utterly inessential? In doing so, we forget what *is* essential: our own wholehearted self-devotion. Our own luminous self-belief. Our own will, offered in service of the precious light we all contain. True love can only blossom when we reprioritize our unique light as the most important source of our needs. This flame is your most precious asset. It is the sacred essence of your soul.

---

55 "The Dangerous Concentration of the Seed Market," Public Eye (Public Eye, 2021), https://www.publiceye.ch/en/topics/seeds/concentration-of-the-seed-market.

No one and no thing you could ever sacrifice yourself for can offer you this.
Place your fire at the center of the altar of your heart. Become its devoted guardian, even in the harshest of winds. Come home to its warmth whenever you feel distracted or lost. Make life-affirming choices that fan the flames of your love.
You are the only one you promised your life to. You didn't come here to please or appease. You came here to light the world on fire."

Camille Willemain,[56] Founder, Earth Daughters, Feminine Embodiment Teacher @camillewillemain @earthdaughters

## CONCLUSION: SEEDS OF LOVE

"We've been infected with this idea that love is an emotion only felt between two people. But love is universal. An energy. A contagious force. A gift. To offer money to a homeless man is to love. To save a worm from the sun is love. To smile at a stranger is love. To be grateful, to be hopeful, to be brave, to be forgiving, to be proud, is to love."

—A. R. Lucas

When it comes to the love within us and surrounding us, it is so important for us to nourish it like a garden, starting at the core of love in our own hearts and rippling

---

56 https://www.earthdaughters.org/.

outwards to the garden surrounding us. We are seeds, ready to sprout and then blossom; it is time for us to remember the love that is our true nature. We all have this seed deep within our hearts. The best way to cultivate our garden of love is to start planting seeds—within ourselves and in the earth—each cycle.

Each new moon and full moon, I like to journal about the opportunities and goals that I would like to plant and see flourish. I write out what I need to burn away and let go and what I want to bring into form. We prune the plants in our garden, making cuttings near the new moon and propagating plants and planting seeds each full moon. I highly recommend planting and propagating both your literal and symbolic gardens with your own seasons and cycles. We can plant seeds of regeneration in the earth with each cycle; we can plant seeds of love within ourselves with intention-setting, positive affirmations, and radical transparency.

∞

### 9/11/2018, San Jose, Costa Rica

*Nature seems most beautiful left untouched. Left wild.*
*I used to believe what society told me about beauty.*
*Masks. Makeup. Skincare needs to start early.*
*Birth control will help regulate your cycles. Eliminate acne.*
*Use products without even knowing what's in them.*

*I changed.*

*We can all make this shift.*

*I learned, little by little.*
*The more I ate directly from the earth, the greater connection*
*I had to my food.*
*My body healed itself. Renewing cells. Shedding skins.*
*Digging. Investigating the core.*
*Child of God. Love.*

*We all have the ability to change. Unlearn.*
*Come back to our pure child, before society started to scar us.*
*Let's break down old systems that don't serve this earth.*
*Let's regenerate ourselves and this planet for our children.*

*Plant seeds for generations to come.*
*Make love—all ways.*

∞

At the core of every being—animal, forest, garden, and human—is a seed of love. May we nourish this love, watering it daily. When we feel darkness, may we ride it like a wave, understanding that everything is impermanent. Since storms don't last forever, may we then enjoy the love that follows even more.

To clear space for our seeds of love to flourish, we also need to release old, cluttered patterns of thought and behavior. When we can acknowledge patterns of suffering within our families and ourselves, we can become an observer, catching this inner dialogue and releasing it as if it were a cloud floating by.

∞

*11/12/2018 Playa Chiquita, Costa Rica*

*Life is all about perspective—*

*The lens through which we see.*
*We all have different perspectives on reality.*
*Versions of history.*
*We must trust our intuition.*
*Seek the truth.*
*Dig like a dog for a bone.*
*Understand the destruction humans have wreaked.*
*The patterns we repeat.*
*Break free.*
*It's not an easy path.*
*It hurts. Feeling everything.*
*Beautiful mess of life.*
*We choose to be the problem or solution.*
*A pathless path. Connecting back to our nature.*
*Love.*

∞

What would your life be like if you knew it was always guided by love?

When we know our life is guided, we trust and surrender to the waves of life, the beauty of impermanence, the mystery of the unknown, the simple moments, and the love that is within us and around us. We attract reflections of ourselves. When we encounter darkness, we recognize it, pray, feel it, and put our intentions out into the universe, knowing it has our back.

We love. We can choose it. We are seeds of love.

"The purpose of life is to spread this joy, happiness, love, goodwill, and blessings everywhere we go, so that when you leave this place the world will be better for your having been here."

—Joshua David Stone, *Soul Psychology*

# Guided Inquiry

### Heart Opening
### Written by Sarah Marie Wu

"One of the most intimate things about self-love is holding your heart in your own hands.
How often I reach to my heart, when I greet people, feel joy, feel sorrow, feel every feel—it's the first place I touch, pretty unconsciously, reminding myself how much love I have to give, that when I keep my heart soft, it can grow and grow and contain the whole universe.

Take a moment to touch your sacred and precious heart and say out loud:

*I am loving kindness.*
*I am loving abundance.*
*I am loving intentions.*
*I am deserving of deep, radical, big love.*
*I am open to interconnected love.*
*Love is my action.*
*Love is my compass.*
*Love is my pure and powerful magic.*
*With love I create.*
*With love I let go.*
*With love I dedicate.*

*With love I operate.*
*With love I take risks.*
*With love I have no fear.*
*With love I offer space.*
*Love is the great healer.*
*Love is a gentle balm.*
*Love is a medicinal elixir.*
*Love is to be nurtured.*
*Love is to be cherished.*
*Love is to be seen.*
*In love I show up.*
*In love I set healthy boundaries.*
*In love I trust.*

*Look at yourself in the mirror and say, "I love you."
*Tell everyone you love how much you love them, and frequently.
*Show them how you love them.
*Tell the earth, "I love you."
*Show the earth how you love it."

# Affirmations

### Introduction written by Joshua David Stone
### (Soul Psychology,
### Chapter 9)[57]

"An affirmation is in reality an attitude. Every thought
you think, be it positive or negative, is an affirmation.
Every word you speak is an affirmation. Every action you
take is an affirmation. This is true because everything
stems from your thoughts. Your thoughts create your
reality."

∞

### How to Reprogram the Subconscious Mind:

Affirmations are statements specifically designed to
program a certain feeling or behavior into your subconscious mind, bringing you back into your higher self
and into your power. We can protect our inner world by
pushing negative thoughts out of our mind; much like
*not* watering a plant, when a thought gets no energy, it
withers and it dies.

---

57 Joshua David Stone, *Soul Psychology: How to Clear Negative Emotions and Spir-
itualize Your Life* (New York, NY: Ballantine Wellspring, Ballantine Pub. Group,
1999).

Write down three affirmations and post them around your home. Each time you see them, read them out loud to yourself. The repetitive use of positive thoughts and affirmations waters the new seed-thought in the soil of your subconscious mind, and new life begins to grow. With the next new moon, plant seeds and repeat these affirmations to yourself. Place your physical seeds somewhere with partial shade and near your home, watering them lightly every day and watching them sprout. After the seedlings grow roots, transplant them into your garden or a larger pot.

## Wisdom Questions

♥ How do my actions and thoughts cultivate love?

♥ What makes me feel most in love with life?

♥ How do I make love to the earth?

# VI
# THE PLANT MEDICINE QUEENDOM

**Affirmation: Plants are my allies. Plants are my medicine. Plants are a Queendom; they connect me to the universe.**

*"Let food be thy medicine, and let medicine be thy food*
*The natural healing force within each of us . . .*
*Everything in excess is opposed by nature."*

—Hippocrates

For the last five years, I have been surrounded by artists, gardeners, permaculturists, herbalists, and lovers of medicine, fungi, and nature. When we gather, we excitedly talk about plants and their uses, often helping each other to heal with plants and herbalism. We share meals crafted from our gardens or our latest tinctures and tea blends.

During these gatherings, I've been like a sponge, learning about different plants and patterns of the forest:

- Rivers are the veins of the earth, similar to our veins.
- Spirals repeat in shells, in plants, and in our lives.

- ◉ The sacred geometric flower of life repeats in psychedelic journeys and in literal flowers.

- ◉ The roots of trees mimic our human lungs, breathing for the earth.

For the last four years, I have often read Ed Bernhardt's *Medicinal Plants of Costa Rica* before bed to get sleepy and learn about the medicinal properties of plants. Alan and I have collected fifty-one of the ninety-two medicinal plants listed in the book. I love reading about how to ally with plants for healing. I like to think of food as medicine, and farmers as doctors.

I remember the first time I read *The Secret Life of Plants* by Peter Tompkins and Christopher Bird. I was thrilled to learn how plants have such a beautiful intelligence and can listen and respond to the environment around them. I love walking through our gardens, observing and singing to the plants. I can feel how their beauty connects me to love, gratitude, and the present moment. It's moving to look at a forest and see how all the different plants and species grow and coexist together.

"Short of Aphrodite, there is nothing lovelier on this planet than a flower, nor more essential than a plant. The true matrix of human life is the green sward covering mother earth. Without green plants we would neither breathe nor eat. On the undersurface of every leaf a million movable lips are engaged in devouring carbon dioxide and expelling oxygen. All together, twenty-five million square miles of leaf surface are daily engaged in this miracle of photosynthesis, producing oxygen and food for man and beast."

—*Secret Life of Plants,*[58] Peter Tompkins and Christopher Bird

The earliest forms of life on earth are plants that have been discovered in fossils dating back 3.2 million years. Plants provided the foundation for the development of all life forms, even animals. They have a beautiful relationship with the sun and the cycles, synthesizing organic compounds that support all of us. Before modern medicine entered the scene, plants *were* our medicine. As much as 40 percent of the drugs behind the pharmacist's counter are derived from plants that people have used for centuries (such as aspirin from willow bark and quinine extracted from the bark of the South American cinchona tree to relieve malaria).[59]

According to Medicinal Botany, the top twenty best-selling prescription drugs come directly from plants.[60] There are thirty-five thousand to seventy thousand medicinal plants that we know of, and many more that we don't know about, and others that we will *never*

---

58 Peter Tompkins and Christopher Bird, *The Secret Life of Plants* (New York, NY: Harper & Row, 1973).

59 "Medicinal Botany," U.S. Forest Service (USDA), accessed November 2, 2021, https://www.fs.fed.us/wildflowers/ethnobotany/medicinal/index.shtml.

60 "Medicinal Botany," U.S. Forest Service (USDA), accessed November 2, 2021, https://www.fs.fed.us/wildflowers/ethnobotany/medicinal/index.shtml.

know about because they are extinct. Many medicines have not made it into modern medicine but are sacred and valuable to so many cultures around the world.

Plants are our allies, and they have been a key part of my personal healing path. Our very survival on this planet depends on them.

## RESILIENCE IN PLANTS

"I would bet that the most resilient and healthiest people in history, those who were able to sustain themselves during mass food shortages and times of war, were very intimate with their landscapes.

They knew the power of the nettles and the seaweed, the vitality in the yarrow and the daisy.

They picked pennywort on their walks and ate it right there under the sky.

They knew the few poisonous plants around them and the medicine in everything else.

I've been thinking lately that all the money we spend as a society on supplements and powders from other parts of the world—how much good do they really do? The plants around us are built for the environment we live in, providing us the medicine we need to also thrive in that specific area.

Certain things seem exotic and rare when they come from far-off places, but I really believe deep resilience comes from eating the things that grow around you. The plant medicine available to your body is perfectly curated wherever you find yourself."

–Katie McCormick[61], Founder of Bloom Like a Mother, Wise Woman Holistic Healing, Ireland, @bloomlikeamother_

In this chapter, I will share some of my favorite plants and the knowledge systems that have supported my personal growth, queendom, happiness, and well-being.

---

### QUEENDOM

I offer the word "Queendom" as an alternative to the more commonplace "Kingdom" in an effort to shift toward a more matriarchal and cyclical way of living. I love to see my fellow sister queens thriving, following their passions, and supporting each other through circular economies. I am creating a reality that is authentic and true to my heart. I am building my own Queendom.

---

Each person has a different path. What is best for me may not be suitable for others. I acknowledge and honor your inner compass. Take from this chapter what resonates with you, and let your heart lead. When we release our inner blocks, we allow ourselves to fully embody our **personal power** and our unique gifts. We each have our own key to unlock this power.

---

61 Bloom Like a Mother, www.bloomlikeamother.com.

## PERSONAL POWER

Our personal power is our ability to influence or change outcomes; it is manifested in our best version of ourselves, when we are moving from our heart with strength and confidence. This power comes from our core, our heart–not from our ego.

## HIGH ON MOUNTAINS

"Digging out plant roots,
walking the path of my own roots.
Foraging mushrooms, wild berries, and admiring
rosehip abundance in my basket.
Spirit whispers and sun embraces.
Wilderness is where I am reborn
and where all mental unrest runs to drown
itself voluntarily in the gurgling springs,
streams, and ponds that emerge behind every curve of this
forest path,
and what used to be a dry meadow now is a lush, green oasis
of singing waters feeding the valley straight from the rocky
hillsides and pointy mountain tops.
Life is a blue-green rhapsody and
I am so blessed to be a Wild,
and not a Tamed, Woman."

–Rea Farout,[62] DJ, Retreats & Events Producer, Workshops
& Wellness Facilitator

---

62 Rea Farout, https://www.mixcloud.com/ReaFarout/farout-sessions-pt3-shades-of-azul/.

## HERBALISM

> "Herbalism is the study and practice of botany, ethnobotany, pharmacology, phytochemistry, biology, chemistry, ecology, anatomy, physiology, pathophysiology, permaculture, farming, gardening, medicine making, cooking, first aid, community health, counseling, psychology, conservation, restoration, activism, alchemy, history, mythology, allegory, storytelling, and for some . . . witchcraft."
>
> —Sarah Marie Wu

As I have learned through my studies, the practice of herbalism starts with a handful of plants that are accessible where we live and then grows as we get to know each plant with grace and experimentation. I started learning about a few plants (such as gotu kola, tilo, cuculmeca, echinacea, and hibiscus, to name a few) and then expanded from there. I continue to learn about the medicinal uses of more varieties, collecting different plants along the way.

I use herbalism each day, tuning in to my body and its needs, and I preventatively take my plant medicines through soups, sauces, teas, ferments, and tinctures. I still believe a balance of modern medicine and herbal medicine is necessary. I just avoid pharmaceutical drugs or synthetic substances unless they are completely necessary, as in the case of a life-threatening emergency.

Most healing must come from within, going to the root of the problem instead of temporarily patching up symptoms until the next warning or dis-ease presents itself. Herbalism isn't only about healing illness; it is also about supporting our day-to-day wellness. During my menstruation, for example, I make myself basil and mint tea. I drink turmeric and ginger every day to keep my body's immunity high. I could go on and on here, but I highly recommend taking courses or reading about a few plants to assemble your own personal apothecary of go-to remedies. Instead of taking pharmaceuticals as soon as you feel unwell, consider looking into herbal remedies and allowing your body to heal with rest and regenerative plant medicines.

The first herbal conference I attended was "Medicines from the Edge" at the Punta Mona educational center on the Caribbean coast of Costa Rica. Sarah Wu, the organizer, gathered all the plant people of the country to share their knowledge in workshops and talks. This is where I met many of my favorite plant teachers, along with the agroforestry experts I work with today.

∞

*10/23/2017 Punta Mona, Costa Rica*

*Leaving refreshed, renewed, reborn from "Medicines from the Edge."*
*Grateful for the grand lessons where the Caribbean waters meet the jungle,*

*grateful for the prayers, the community, the web of*
*connections,*
*the collective consciousness,*
*the plants, ancestors, and the heart of the project (the*
*kitchen).*
*Ready to keep on the path,*
*knowing there are so many ways to reach the same divine*
*source.*

∞

Herbalism is a beautiful knowledge system that has greatly enhanced my life. Oftentimes, it is only the grandmothers who still have this plant knowledge. There is a generational gap all over the world because in modern cultures, education about natural medicine is uncommon, and young people are not learning about the natural world.

In addition, it is arguably not in the best interest of the pharmaceutical industry for people to heal themselves. It is more profitable for corporations if we stay sick, spend more on healthcare, and stimulate the economy. In a study on the business of illness, researchers suggested that "pharmaceutical companies sponsor diseases and promote them to prescribers and consumers."[63] Revenue from the global pharmaceutical industry has grown exponentially from 2001 to 2019. In 2001, the market was

---

63 Ray Moynihan, Iona Heath, and David Henry, "Selling Sickness: The Pharmaceutical Industry and Disease Mongering," *BMJ* 324, no. 7342 (2002): pp. 886-891, https://doi.org/10.1136/bmj.324.7342.886.

valued at just $390 billion USD, and in 2019 at $1.25 trillion USD.[64] The United States has emerged as the leading market for pharmaceuticals—and fear-based media production. It is important to become aware of the role that the media, corporations, and governments play when it comes to dis-ease and fear:

> "The social construction of illness is being replaced by the corporate construction of disease . . . . A key strategy of the alliances is to target the news media with stories designed to create fears about the condition or disease and draw attention to the latest treatment. Company sponsored advisory boards supply the 'independent experts' for these stories, consumer groups provide the 'victims,' and public relations companies provide media outlets with the positive spin about the latest 'breakthrough' medications."[65]

By applying herbalism in my everyday life as preventative care, I discovered that I could take the power of health and healing back into my own hands. I have realized that I am a healer, as are you! We have the ability to heal ourselves through herbalism and conscious consumption.

---

64 Matej Mikulic, "Global Pharmaceutical Market Size 2001-2019," Statista, May 4, 2021, https://www.statista.com/statistics/263102/pharmaceutical-market-world-wide-revenue-since-2001/.

65 Ray Moynihan, Iona Heath, and David Henry, "Selling Sickness: The Pharmaceutical Industry and Disease Mongering," *BMJ* 324, no. 7342 (2002): pp. 886-891, https://doi.org/10.1136/bmj.324.7342.886.

We build our sovereignty, day by day, by mindfully culti-vating our gardens and our body temples.

## CACAO

Cacao is my favorite plant medicine! Most of my family would say, "You mean chocolate?" No, I mean *cacao*, a sa-cred fruit that grows on trees. Its scientific name is *Theo-broma cacao*, which means "food of the gods." Originating in the Americas, growing all the way from the Amazon to the south of Mexico, cacao thrives in diverse ecosystems with many different companion plants (including ginger, cardamon, cinnamon, bananas, and breadfruit). Cacao can play an important role in regenerating our planet at the level of environment, society, economy, culture, and community.[66] Many indigenous cultures in the Ameri-cas used cacao for thousands of years as currency, food, drink, and many other sacred functions.

When we come together and share cacao, we open our hearts to the deeper potential of cultivating harmo-ny within ourselves, with each other, and in the relation-ships we have with everything. Personally, I like to sip cacao for extra inspiration in art, writing, or singing in ceremonies.

The real cacao ceremony includes all aspects of the value chain—from growing and harvesting to processing. The celebration occurs when we consume the cacao, con-nect to its source, and get to know the hands that make

66 Scott Gallant, "Syntropic Agriculture: Cacao, Costa Rica, Case Study," Regeneration International (April 8, 2021), https://regenerationinternational.org/2021/04/08/syntropic-agriculture-cacao-costa-rica-case-study/.

our cacao dreams possible. The cacao ceremony begins with growing and caring for the trees until it is time to harvest the fruits.

## HOW TO MAKE CACAO

After breaking the cacao shell open, nibble off the sweet fruit that surrounds the seeds, imprinting your natural bacteria to start the fermentation process. Traditionally, the seeds are then wrapped in banana leaves to ferment for five days. Next, dry the cacao in the sun for three to five days, depending on the climate. Then lightly toast the beans over a fire, moving them slowly until the skins begin to crack. Remove the skins by hand and fan away the remaining shells and debris. Once the cacao beans are deshelled, they are traditionally hand-ground with stones. Then the pure cacao is poured into molds to set, or turned into chocolate with sugar or other ingredients.

Cacao is used as medicine in various spiritual and healing-oriented ceremonies. When we consume it with the intention of healing or opening the heart, cacao has tremendous potential for doing some profound work. From a scientific standpoint, cacao is a food that is naturally high in magnesium, "the relaxer mineral," which softens tissues, relaxes muscles, and eases tension. When we ingest a medicinal dose of cacao (around forty grams), the magnesium goes to the heart first, physically helping to release tension and constriction.[67] These physical

---

67 David L Katz, Kim Doughty, and Ather Ali, "Cocoa and Chocolate in Human Health and Disease," Antioxidants & Redox Signaling (Mary Ann Liebert, Inc., November 15, 2011), https://www.ncbi.nlm.nih.gov/pmc/articles/PMC4696435/.

effects can also have a softening, energetic effect on what is known in yogic philosophy as the "heart chakra."[68]

"Cacao is a medicine for everybody, as it has the capacity to balance every system in our bodies. It affects each one of us differently; it speeds or relaxes our metabolism, stabilizes fluctuating moods, enhances fertility, and so on. Drinking a large amount of cacao increases the heart and brain activity by 30–40 percent, and opens blockages of all sorts— physical and emotional."

—Eva Dalak

∞

*4/16/2017 Mystical Yoga Farm, Guatemala*

*Yoga teacher training, cacao ceremony, journaling on intentions.*
*When we set our intentions, mine was to continue to be reborn and embrace change—*
*to be my authentic self, full of love and abundance,*
*stripping away everything that doesn't serve me,*
*to trust,*
*to flow,*
*and to feel the oneness of all.*

---

68 Zahrah Sita, "Heart Opening Cacao Ceremonies," The Costa Rica News, January 8, 2021, https://thecostaricanews.com/cacao-ceremonies/.

*To follow my heart's path.*
*To be.*

*I feel like I have unlocked and unleashed my hummingbird*
*spirit and sweetness, rapid thoughts of possibilities that are*
*becoming my reality.*

∞

I love cacao as a source of magical inspiration. As I write this chapter, I am sipping cacao and looking out at our perennial garden. I feel inspired and full of love and hope. I highly recommend creating your own cacao ceremony and discovering your own inspiration with the exercise at the end of this chapter.

## MARIJUANA

Folk history in India maintains that the gods sent the hemp plant to earth to share more delight and courage. The legend of marijuana tells that a magical nectar dropped from the heavens and cannabis sprouted from it.[69] This plant ally has been with humanity for at least ten thousand years, since the dawn of the Agricultural Age. The hemp plant has five primary uses (and many more secondary ones):

1. Textile use through hemp fiber.

---

69 Richard Evans Schultes, Albert Hofmann, and Rätsch Christian, *Plants of the Gods: Their Sacred, Healing and Hallucinogenic Powers* (Rochester, VT: Healing Arts Press, 2006).

2. Skin problem and stress alleviation through hemp oil.

3. Protein-rich food through hemp seeds.

4. Narcotic properties through hemp flowers.

5. Therapeutic applications for a wide spectrum of illnesses.

Throughout history, cannabidiol (CBD) and marijuana have been utilized as a cure-all. In Tibetan Buddhism, which originated in the Himalayan region, cannabis sometimes plays a significant role in ritual as well, used to facilitate deep meditation and awareness.

Today, things have changed. Marijuana has become an excuse for racial and classist discrimination in many parts of the world. For example, in the US, legal policies are enforced inconsistently, disproportionately targeting Black and Latino populations. In 1971, President Nixon declared drug abuse to be "public enemy number one." Present-day articles on the topic claim that "the policies that his administration implemented as part of the Comprehensive Drug Abuse Prevention and Control Act of 1970 are still with us today."[70]

John Ehrlichman, Watergate co-conspirator, told *Harper's Magazine,* "We knew we couldn't make it illegal to be either against the war or black, but by getting

71 Andrew Glass, "Reagan Declares 'War on Drugs,' October 14, 1982," POLITICO (Politico LLC, October 14, 2010), https://www.politico.com/story/2010/10/reagan-declares-war-on-drugs-october-14-1982-043552.

the public to associate the hippies with marijuana and blacks with heroin, and then criminalizing both heavily, we could disrupt those communities."[71]

I believe that marijuana should be legalized and that anyone put in prison for marijuana possession or marijuana-related "crimes" should be released. I have directly benefited from the use of cannabis, as have many people close to me. I remember the last time I smoked with my mom, who was suffering from cancer, and the way it eased both of our pains. This medicine has helped me dance through the hard times of my mother's passing, aided my sleep, and helped me manage anxiety and come into the present moment. Marijuana is an ancient, sacred plant that should be respected and used with intention.

Marijuana has been a plant ally through different cycles of my life. It has inspired me to be braver, channel songs, and connect with the elements of fire, water, air, and earth on a deep, spiritual level. I remember once setting the intention of connecting with a tree and meditating at the base of its giant roots. I truly felt a connection to the years of wisdom and carbon it had drawn down; breathing with the tree, I could fully appreciate the fresh air it helped to create.

Marijuana is not for everyone. However, when taken with intention and in moderation, I believe that cannabis can be a plant ally to many, curing ailments and supporting wellness.

---

71 Dan Baum, "Legalize It All: How to Win the War on Drugs," Harper's Magazine, March 31, 2016, https://harpers.org/archive/2016/04/legalize-it-all/.

## HALLUCINOGENIC PLANT MEDICINES

As I traveled through Mexico, Guatemala, and Costa Rica in 2016 and 2017, different plant medicines entered into my field of consciousness. I learned about how various cultures use hallucinogenic plants to expand their minds and heal themselves. Before changing my lifestyle, I was afraid to try any hallucinogenic plant medicines because I was afraid to give up control. Society told me that these are the "bad drugs" and that pharmaceutical drugs are the "good drugs." I was afraid that my trip would be too long or that I would never come back to myself. I didn't know what to expect. I couldn't even imagine shifting into a different dimension and surrendering control.

Historically, our society has shamed natural medicines and psychedelics, recommending only modern pharmaceutical solutions. It's exciting to see this starting to shift, as is the case with research on the use of psychedelics in treating depression and addiction, promoted by Paul Stamets and Michael Pollan in popular books. Hallucinogenic plant medicines can help expand the pineal gland, create new neural pathways, and address emotional or psychological problems at the root. In the documentary *DMT: The Spirit Molecule*, people describe the experience of N-Dimethyltryptamine (DMT) as being like "breaking out of a simulation."

"People report being able to access the true inner workings of their minds, and describe the feeling of being launched into other dimensions, where they experience their consciousness existing outside of their own bodies."

—Lindsay Dodgson, *Business Insider*

In my own experience, hallucinogenic plant medicines have significantly supported my understanding of the universe and my sense of connection to Source.

---

### SOURCE

Source is a word frequently used to describe an esoteric sense of the unknown, a divine spirit, or "something" out there that is bigger than ourselves. Some may prefer words such as God, love, or a divine connection to the universe.

---

As described in *Plants of the Gods*, "These psychic changes and unusual states of consciousness induced by hallucinogens are so far removed from similarity with ordinary life that it is scarcely possible to describe them in the language of daily living." This quote resonates with me so much because I also struggle to put words to my experience. I still try, though, because I think it is important to talk about it.

I do not recommend hallucinogens to everyone because it's a highly personal decision. Each person has to navigate their own feelings about these substances (opinions tied to science, politics, society) and make up their own mind about what is "good" and "bad." I don't necessarily promote utilizing hallucinogens; however, in my own personal experience, they have greatly supported my health when I have taken them with caution and in safe environments. A few memorable occasions have led me to value plant medicines as a complement to the deep inner work of releasing mental blocks, old stories, and traumas, and viewing the universe as magical and full of love.

Below I will share a few hallucinogens that came into my path and supported my health and well-being.

## Wachuma (San Pedro)

Wachuma, also known as San Pedro, is a sacred cactus native to the Andean Mountains. San Pedro is one of Peru's most sacred plants and has been used for over four thousand years to heal and expand consciousness. It is mostly consumed in powder form in teas or capsules. It is extremely bitter and can cause mild nausea initially. This medicine enhances all the senses, connecting us to Source, to nature, and to the universe.

∞

### 1/30/2017 El Paredon, Guatemala

*We took a boat ride down a river of mangrove trees at 7 a.m.,
watching the sunrise, the reflection of the mangroves on the
water, and the sun peeking through the trees.
I cried in joy watching condors and hawks by the dozen*

*circling above us, like our spirits bringing our hearts high,*
*higher than the clouds.*

*When we finished our boat ride, we jumped into the ocean for*
*a baptism;*
*the waves felt like orgasms brushing over me.*
*I was rolling, floating, moving with the ocean—heightened*
*sensation,*
*the colors of the sun on the waves,*
*the water christening me felt like heaven.*

∞

I feel that the medicine of San Pedro is still with me, as it permanently opened me up to a more colorful and vibrant way of seeing things. It enhanced my perspective, my sensitivity, and my connection to love. In those moments I described in my journal, I was not thinking; I was just being, in my purest essence. It was a profound experience of feeling connected to myself, to my partner, and to the universe. "Being" is a state of free-flow, a creative state of unconditional love. I felt my interconnectedness to all life, and I became more aware of the nectar flowing through us all.

San Pedro is not for everyone and must be taken in the right environment. As a starting point to learn more about San Pedro and other plant medicines, I highly recommend reading *Plants of the Gods*. (You can find my full recommended documentary and reading lists at the end of this book.)

## Mushrooms

For the last ten thousand years, humans have consumed *psilocybin*, the naturally occurring psychedelic compound in "magic" (hallucinogenic) mushrooms. Mushrooms became popularized partly because of a visit made by J. P. Morgan's R. Gordon Wasson and the Beatles to María Sabina. María was from Oaxaca, Mexico, and was well-respected in her village as a healer and shaman. "Seeking the Magic Mushroom," a *Life Magazine* article written about Wasson's visit to María and the first recorded encounter with mushrooms, went 1957-viral upon its publication.[72] María describes mushroom ceremonies as a communion with God to heal the sick.

I didn't try mushrooms until I was thirty. I was afraid because of other people's stories, or my own worries that my journey would last too long. Basically, I was afraid of losing control.

∞

### 2/27/2018, Envision Festival, Mystical Tea Lounge, Costa Rica

*My intention was to elevate my already-happy state,*
*to let the medicine do what it needed to do.*
*In the Mystical Tea Lounge at Envision Festival, a few friends*
*who were hosting the space served me tea and water as I*
*journeyed on mushrooms.*

---

72 Ahmed Kabil, "This Mexican Medicine Woman Hipped America to Magic Mushrooms, with the Help of a Bank Executive," Timeline (Medium, January 6, 2017), https://timeline.com/with-the-help-of-a-bank-executive-this-mexican-medicine-woman-hipped-america-to-magic-mushrooms-c41f866bbf37.

*I sat for hours gazing up at the colorful artwork and sunshine
coming through.*
*The hostesses of the space wore cat ears, smiling and meowing
and communicating telepathically, somehow knowing exactly
what I needed.*

*I did not talk; I just recharged.*
*Listening to all the conversations, I received entertainment
and lessons all at the same time.*
*I felt like I was hearing all the conversations at the same
time—as an open-hearted witness.*
*The download rejuvenated my spirit.*
*I felt extreme joy.*

*Life is but a dream.*
*And we ask ourselves, how did we get here?*

∞

In Michael Pollan's recent book, *How to Change Your Mind,* he presents new research on the therapeutic effects of psychedelics.[73] He explains findings that substances such as Lysergic acid diethylamide (LSD) and psilocybin (the active ingredient in magic mushrooms) can help to alleviate depression, anxiety, and addiction—among other ailments. Pollan also met with terminally ill patients who had consumed large doses of these substances and then found themselves to be happy and at peace.[74]

---

73 Michael Pollan, *How to Change Your Mind: The New Science of Psychedelics* (London: Penguin Books, 2019).
74 "Magic Mushrooms, Micro-Dosing and Michael Pollan," ABC Radio (Australian Broadcasting Corporation, July 15, 2020), https://www.abc.net.au/radio/programs/conversations/michael-pollan/12409704.

In my own experiences, I have found mushrooms to be a powerful mental healer. They have helped me connect to my inner knowing and personal power. Mushrooms have allowed me to deeply tap into my inner child, remembering and recreating different fairy spots and fantasy worlds in the jungle. I have had deep belly laughs and moments of inspiration while walking through the forest or rolling in the grass. The mushrooms I have consumed are native to the land; we come across them as we walk through nearby cow pastures.

In addition, Pollan describes how "set and setting" can shape our experience of psychedelics. Each time I go on a mushroom journey, I make sure that I am in nature and in a safe environment for me to be me. If there are people around, they are supporting me and encouraging me to let out my inner child. Thanks to proper set and setting, I have experienced profound healing with mushrooms. I tend to be very sensitive to psychedelics, and so I typically choose to microdose with intention in safe, calm settings.

As with all plant medicines, mushrooms are not for everyone and must be taken in the right environment.

## Ayahuasca

After my mom's passing, Grandmother Ayahuasca came to me while I was in my thirty-first sun year. This medicine is made from a jungle vine known as *Banisteriopsis caapi* and a shrub called chacruna, or *Psychotria viridis*, which contains the hallucinogenic substance DMT. The ayahuasca that I drank was grown and brewed at a local farm on the Caribbean coast of Costa Rica.

Ayahuasca is traditionally consumed in the Amazonian and Andean regions of South America. The bitter drink has an intoxicating effect ranging from pleasant and vivid visions with no "hangover" to nausea and purging. The experience typically ends with deep sleep or "waking dreaming." The Colombian *taitas* (spiritual leaders) say that this vine can help cure mental illness and deep wounds or traumas. It is a serpent vine that helps pass important information about the jungle to all beings.

> "Entheogens such as Ayahuasca could be the appropriate medicine for hyper-materialistic humanity on the threshold of the new millennium, where it will be decided if our way will be continuing to grow and progress or if we will be destroyed in a massive biological holocaust unparalleled by anything that has happened in our realm in the last 65 million years . . . "
>
> —*Plants of the Gods*, Richard Evans Schultes, Albert Hofmann, and Christian Ratsch[75]

---

75 Richard Evans Schultes, Albert Hofmann, and Rätsch Christian, *Plants of the Gods: Their Sacred, Healing and Hallucinogenic Powers* (Rochester , VT: Healing Arts Press, 2006).

During my first ceremony, as the Ayahuasca brew was being prepared, I set the intention to feel love and connection to Mother Earth—and to my own mother. During my experience, I felt deeply connected to myself and the earth. I felt total clarity that I was (and am) on my heart's path. During my journey, I saw all tribes joining hands in harmony with the earth. After my journey, I became fascinated with the **Rainbow Prophecy,** which refers to the keepers of the legends, rituals, and other myths that will be needed when the time comes to regenerate the earth:[76]

> "It is believed that these legendary beings [Rainbow Warriors] will return on a day of awakening, when all people will unite and create a new world of justice, peace, and freedom, and they will be named the 'Warriors of the Rainbow.' They will reteach the values and the knowledge that have been lost in time, demonstrating how to have wisdom and extra-perception, and how unity, harmony, and love are the only way forward."[77]
>
> —The Rainbow Prophecy

"As Native Americans, we believe the Rainbow is a sign from the Spirit in all things. It is a sign of the

---

76 "Earth Needs Rainbow Warriors," Octopus (Octopus Ages - Regeneration Society, January 21, 2020), https://www.octopusages.com/earth-needs-rainbow-warriors/.

77 Jenni Giovanetti, "Rainbow Warriors," Lakota Times, February 24, 2018, https://www.lakotatimes.com/articles/rainbow-warriors/.

union of all people, like one big family. The unity of all humanity, many tribes, and peoples is essential."

—Thomas Banyacya, Hopi Leader

∞

### 4/23/2019, Playa Chiquita, Costa Rica

*The beginning of a new chapter.*
*Rainbows.*
*Opening the dimensions.*
*Unexplainable to the human mind.*
*A journey to the jungle with the cosmos.*
*Intentions of letting go of expectations.*
*Transforming fear to love.*
*Observing love.*
*Letting go to flow.*
*Surrendering to the lady vine of Ayahuasca,*
*too many histories to describe.*
*A universe going in and out of Bliss or nothingness,*
*Life energy,*
*her path led me to the divinity of all,*
*the orchestra, the jungle, the vibration of feeling alive.*
*Reconnecting with my mother in the stars.*
*Mother Earth nurturing me—*
*all the medicine.*
*Envisioning harmony.*
*This medicine helps us remember:*
*We are the "Rainbow Warriors."*

∞

I reconnected with my mother as if we were paddle-boarding through the stars together. I cried in joy and sadness and purged out many deeply-rooted emotions and conflicts within me. I am grateful that I had this opportunity to take part in plant medicine healing shortly after my mother's passing. It helped me connect to the divine matriarch in myself, and also cherish the friendship of my sisters. During my ceremony, I envisioned a culture of living in harmony with nature.

Ayahuasca is an incredibly intense experience and requires supervision during the journey and integration afterwards. It is not to be taken lightly. And of course, it is not for everyone and must be consumed in the right environment.

## CONCLUSION: THE PLANT MEDICINE QUEENDOM

Plants are our greatest allies. An entire Queendom of plants and life surrounds us, and it has the power to restore the health and wealth of our communities and planet. Plant medicine and herbalism play a significant role in my everyday life. I love to nourish my garden, harvest fresh herbs, and produce my own medicinal products and foods every day.

The most important aspect of consuming any plant-based food or medicine is to infuse intention into it—and to know where it came from. The intentions we have and the sources we choose for our foods will be personal, just like our path with plant medicine. Each person has a divine path. What is best for me may not be best for others.

You have your own inner compass. Follow that intuition, and let your heart lead.

Plant medicines have helped me to release significant mental and emotional blocks. They have allowed me to explore different realms of awareness, shaping my understanding of the universe. During a few journeys, I felt that I was able to heal ancestral wounds, reconnect with persons who had passed, and sustain deep feelings of love and connectivity.

If you want to carelessly try something new to alter your state of consciousness, do not do it. If you feel called to try a particular hallucinogenic plant medicine on your path, I highly recommend finding an experienced facilitator to aid you along your journey. For me, an experienced facilitator needs to have studied where their plant medicine is grown and the culture it is rooted in, and they need to have experimented with the medicine they serve. Use your intuition to decide what is best for you. I feel that plant medicine was just a step in my healing journey. It continues to come to me in critical times of deep healing.

Plants carry the knowledge that comes with being some of the earliest forms of life on earth. May we honor plants as the solution to bringing back biodiversity to our lands and healing our bodies and minds.

# Guided Inquiry

## Cacao Ceremony
### Introduction written by Ciara Lemony

(I recommend finding a block of raw cacao made from the highest-quality ingredients and hopefully traceable all the way back to the hands that cultivated it and the forests where it grew.)

∞

"If cacao feels at all interesting to you, it is quite likely that the spirit of this beautiful plant medicine is already speaking to you through the pages of this book.

Create a personal ceremony—just you and Cacao, to hear what she might have to say.

Start by pouring two cups of water into a pot. Turn on the stove and become aware of your breathing while the water begins to boil.

As the water boils, prepare yourself a space to chop your block of cacao. Using unroasted cacao is a special option for ceremony. It is minimally processed and contains so much of the plant's true essence.
Before chopping, hold the block of cacao in your hands

for a few moments. Bring it to your nose to slowly inhale the rich aroma. Then, finely chop about two tablespoons' worth of cacao. When the water has reached a boil, keep the pot on the stove but turn off the heat.

Now allow any song that expresses gratitude to spill from your lips as you begin to add the chopped pieces of cacao to the hot pot of water. It can be any song of thanks, even one that you make up in the moment. Singing with a pure intention is what matters.

Once the cacao is fully mixed in with the water, pour yourself a cup and find a quiet place to sit alone, out in nature if possible.

The purpose of a cacao ceremony is essentially to connect with the "spirit" or "energy" of the cacao plant. There are infinite ways to do this. Sipping your cup very slowly, breathing deeply, and noticing how you feel as you drink is a good place to start.

You might like to make your space feel more ceremonial by lighting a candle, saying a prayer, or burning incense.

At some point in your ceremony, ask yourself what your intention is for creating this ceremony today. It may not be obvious.

Take a moment to think and feel . . .

Maybe your intention comes from pure curiosity. Perhaps you set an intention for healing, or to ask for guidance, to remember your true essence, to manifest something in your life, to feel deeper love, to be more spacious, to let go, to be joyful, to check in, to get closer to Nature, to make a nurturing space, to create magic, to commune with the Divine.

Connect with your own reasons for having a ceremony by closing your eyes and relaxing. Listen to your own inner guidance to know what you should do in your ceremony and what it should look like.

Maybe you'd like to experiment with journaling, dancing, singing, stretching, playing an instrument, brainstorming, talking yourself through an issue, observing Nature, sitting in silence, meditating, or creating art.

Open yourself to the spontaneous inspiration, heightened awareness, and expansive freedom that can arise when you create a sacred space of ceremony with cacao.

Allow yourself to enjoy in whichever way you like.

After about ninety minutes, close your ceremonial space. Extend gratitude once again to the cacao plant, to the earth for providing the plant, to the farmers who look after and harvest the fruits, to the many people who make ceremonial cacao available to the world, and to yourself for connecting to this plant medicine in a respectful way.

Even when your ceremony has finished, Cacao continues to speak to your energy and to your spirit. After this ceremony, a door between you and the plant world is opened and a relationship is formed.

As with all of our relationships, our relationship with Cacao thrives with nourishment, love, attention, and respect. If you want to strengthen your relationship with Cacao, listen to the subtle and unique ways that she shows up in your life, continue to drink ceremonially if you feel called (each time tastes and feels different), ask the plant your questions, be creative in how you use her gifts, and practice giving and receiving her medicine in a reciprocal way.

May you use cacao, the food of the Gods, the elixir of Love, as a mirror to remind you of all that you are."

## Wisdom Questions

- ♥ What medicinal plants grow near you?

- ♥ How do you ally with plants in your day-to-day life?

- ♥ Have you considered studying herbalism?

# VII
# DEATH, BACTERIA, & FUNGI

**Affirmation: I embrace death, rebirth, and the cycles of life. I know I am made of many bacteria and fungi. I am a living, live organism. I am vibrantly alive.**

*"I am of the earth*
*And to the earth I shall return once more*
*Life and death are old friends*
*And I am the conversation between them."*

—Rupi Kaur

My mom was diagnosed with stage IV ovarian cancer when I turned twenty-two. She was not expected to live much longer. However, she had a heroine's journey of battles and lived many more magical moments for many more years. My mom was considered the health nut of our family; she was training for a half-marathon when we discovered she had cancer.

We learned about our family's genetics and the patterns of DNA being passed down. My mom was found to have a BRCA2 gene mutation, which allowed other family members to be tested. This family crisis helped wake us up in many other ways, too. It forever changed our perspectives on the value of life, our lifestyle choices, and our chosen paths.

I quickly learned from my mom's illness that life is too short not to live it to our heart's fancy. My mother went through a roller coaster of health and sickness. After ten years of fighting cancer, she was ready to leave this world with grace.

In March of 2018, I flew back to my mama, back to Seattle, and back to my childhood home from Costa Rica. Within twenty-four hours of my journey home, she transformed.

∞

### 3/7/2018 Tacoma, Washington
### (Eve of International Women's Day)

*In the morning my mom says, "Jean, today I'm ready."*
*I say, "Mom, I know. We will let you go."*
*She says, "Jean, sing more," and we listen to all the tunes.*
*We have a concert. The sound lets us go deep.*

*It seems like an entire year in a day.*

*Cycles short and long, sad and happy,*
*beautiful and full of love for life.*
*My family is all together at home.*
*We massage and comfort Mama, hugging her or feeling her heart.*
*The process of life passing is mystical.*
*The day is exactly how God intended.*

*We are divinely here, right on the path.*
*We are angels.*

*The transformation—*
*We open the window, her spirit flies so gently, gracefully*
*fluttering*
*like a blue morpho.*
*We weep.*
*We sob.*
*We hug.*

∞

### 3/18/2018 Puyallup, Washington

### Memorial Words

*I feel you, woman.*
*I feel you, Mama.*
*All the superwomen all over the planet,*
*changing the world.*
*Losing my Mama, being Mama, protecting Mama.*
*The dualities are so hard and beautiful at the same time.*
*Bring the family closer. One.*

*My mom passed the night before International Women's Day.*
*It wasn't by accident. She is passing her life. Crowning mine—*
*ours.*
*I know it is all divine.*

Death, Bacteria, & Fungi

*She is transitioning to unconditional love.*
*Resting peacefully. An angel. A spirit. In me, with me.*
*I feel the prayers, the love. From all the beings all around me.*

*Mom, how can I ever express my gratitude to you?*
*You blessed my life. You made my life.*
*From love. From Joy. I love you.*
*We had an incredible relationship.*
*Mother, best friend, sister, grandmother.*

*You embodied love.*
*We created a life so that*
*most days, before noon,*
*had already been the best day of our lives.*

*Your perception of reality, seeing the art of every moment—*
*You saw light in everything.*
*You were chasing sunshine, brown booby birds,*
*always an adventurer.*
*You lived life to the fullest.*

*You taught me that experiences are much more valuable than*
*material stuff.*
*I'll never forget you teaching me how to advocate for myself:*
*Do not be afraid to ask.*
*Do not be afraid to shoot for a goal and miss.*
*When rejected, try again.*
*Be persistent.*
*Don't take "no" personally.*
*You are a great sage to me.*
*You always told me I am enough.*

*We are enough.*

*Mom, you are the most beautiful woman in the world.*

*Mom, the way you loved Dad taught me about Love.*
*You took time alone, special time, just you two.*
*You served each other, had a romance all your life.*
*I couldn't ask for a better example of caring, fun, and freedom*
*than what you taught me.*

*How can words ever express my love, admiration, gratitude?*

*My brother and I are the luckiest children in the world.*
*To be made from you and Dad.*
*To have a mother like you.*
*You were always there.*
*You designed your life to be in the home.*
*To raise your children.*
*All while having your business. Your passion. Your art.*

*When I learned that you said, "This is the best day of my life"*
*every day to Grandma Fay when you were a little girl, I knew*
*your spirit lived within me too.*

*We create this life. Your perception of life is beautiful.*

∞

After experiencing my mother's passing, our entire family grew together during this special time. I believe that death is merely a transformation. Her love and magical heart live on through us, and nature reminds us of her beauty every day.

## CELEBRATING DEATH AS A BEAUTIFUL CYCLE OF LIFE

The fear of death in Western culture is paralyzing. Most people fear death so much they can't live fully. Our approach to dealing with death has been essentialized down to a sad song, wearing black for mourning, and rejecting this part of life.

I was very afraid of it. The death of a relationship. The death of a past self. The death of loved ones. I couldn't imagine living without my mother, who was my best friend. After working with this fear by practicing Vipassana meditation, studying yogic philosophy, and exploring the Mexican tradition of *Día de los Muertos* (Day of the Dead), I realized something important. The way death had been portrayed to me when I was growing up was not the only reality.

Death is a beautiful transformation of energy. My mom's memorial was a celebration of love, life, colors, and art. My mom had already told the pastor the theme: Grace and Love. Now that she has transformed, I remember her and speak with her in different mediums. Sometimes I journal a message for my mom or my grandfather. I pray and talk with passed ones by speaking to them in nature. I have found that the best way to reach this connection is to go to a special spot in nature and tune into all the beauty surrounding me. I come into my breath and the present.

If you would like to explore this kind of connection with those who have transformed, some possibilities include praying, journaling, singing, or silently connecting with their spirits through nature. Another path is to start breathing deeply, listening to the sounds and songs of nature, and allowing yourself to cry and release. It feels great to remember loved ones and feel them through different tools and mediums.

Other times, special people come into my life as divine, feminine women who channel the "Mama energy." I came straight back to Costa Rica after my mother's passing. My dear sister Astaria Light supported my grieving process there; she held me in floating water therapy and sang, "I love you. Mama is holding you. You are safe."

Whenever I encounter it, this divine feminine energy helps me connect to my mother's love. My sisters' music and words connect me to the Mother Nature who resides within me.

"Death is nothing else but going home to God, the bond of love will be unbroken for all eternity."
—Mother Teresa

My family spread my mother's ashes in many different gardens, mountains, and bodies of water. The image of ashes floating out into the universal waters reminds me that floating in water is always a happy place of connecting to her and to myself. Water cleanses me of sadness and brings me into a feeling of being held in the womb of creation. By connecting with nature, I connect with her—and all.

∞

*4/9/2018 Playa Chiquita, Costa Rica*

*Closing cycles.*
*Letting life flow.*
*Ceremony.*
*Sunrise. Rain. Snuggles. Yoga. Adventure day to Finca Isla we go.*
*A hike through the food forest hunting for rare fruit.*
*Trying different colors, flavors of the rainbow.*
*Saving the seeds.*

*In the afternoon, my family spreads my mother's ashes on our garden and all of our fruit trees, starting with the cacao, papayas, avocados, and breadfruit.*
*Fairy dust bringing life back and connecting again with Mother—*
*my hands feel the network of mycelium running.*
*We go to the Caribbean waters; we say a prayer of letting go, putting some of the ashes back into the ocean.*
*Then at night we go to a cacao ceremony, opening and expressing ourselves.*
*Singing and dancing,*
*I feel a rainbow shining from my heart,*

*all the way to the roots, feeling each mantra sound of the*
*universe.*
*A love ceremony from Mother. A complete cycle returning to*
*unconditional love.*

∞

It was a full cycle of life, rebirth, and celebration in a day, spreading my mother's ashes in the garden and celebrating with ceremony at night. When I faced death and accepted it, the fear melted away. Death is a key part of the cycle of life; we should honor and embrace it just as much as birth.

In fact, death *becomes* rebirth through the soils of our gardens, bringing nutrients to the earth, and nourishing new life.

"What a caterpillar calls the end of the world we call a butterfly."

—Eckhart Tolle, *The Power of Now: A Guide to Spiritual Enlightenment*

## CYCLES OF LIFE & REBIRTH

My mother's death helped me see how precious this life is. It showed me that death can happen at any time in our lives and that it will eventually come for all. Death is the ultimate teacher, and if we're listening, it calls us to wake up. Coming to an acceptance of death helped me dismantle my life—letting one way of life die and supporting my transformation to the next.

We can live many lifetimes within the same life, and experience many little ego deaths along the way. Even with the cycles of the seasons or our menstrual cycles, we go through life and rebirth. Each time we rise out of the depths of darkness, we gain more strength. Thanks to the darkness, we are able to appreciate moments of illumination even more.

We can decompose and bloom again. Sometimes we even transform in a day:

∞

### 9/23/2018 Playa Chiquita, Costa Rica

*Death to rebirth*
*in an instant.*
*A full cycle in a day.*
*From death to transition,*
*tears, blood, sweat, fear,*
*doubt, love, joy, aliveness, and self-care.*
*When I stop planning,*

*I stay in the present, and magic happens.*
*If I fall into the conditioning that tells me I need to plan and*
*control the future,*
*the expectations make me sick.*
*Everything can change in an instant.*
*your life can flip and flop turning upside down,*
*erupt in burning.*

*We are strong.*
*If shit hits the fan,*
*life's beautiful mess is splashed out.*

*Tell it how it is.*
*Let the plan raincheck.*
*Let the natural cycle happen,*
*the patterns that repeat in all of it.*
*My day went from sadness at human misery,*
*lack of hope in humanity,*

*to circling with women, seeing my mirrors,*
*knowing we can do it.*
*We are not alone.*

*This is bigger than any individual—*
*a collective shift.*
*New Earth reprogramming.*
*From dark to light again.*

∞

Although I have come to accept death, that doesn't mean I don't have moments of sadness, joy, and tears remembering the woman who birthed me. However, in my experience, once we are able to accept that we will all die, and that it could be at any time, then we can truly live. We can release the crippling fear of death. We can live our lives to the fullest, knowing that each moment is precious.

> "Watch any plant or animal and let it teach you
> acceptance of what is, surrender to the Now.
> Let it teach you Being.
> Let it teach you integrity—which means to be one,
> to be yourself, to be real.
> Let it teach you how to live and how to die, and
> how not to make living and dying into a problem."
> —Eckhart Tolle, *The Power of Now: A Guide to
> Spiritual Enlightenment*

All organisms die and transform, rebirthing into new forms. When a tree falls from the winds and storms, it decomposes, becoming part of the mycelium network of fungi, creating new soil, and causing seeds to bloom into new life. We are currently witnessing a time of transition in the world. With overpopulation, deforestation, extractive industries, species collapse, factory fishing and farming, viruses, and global warming will come a collective rebirth into a new way of being.

"The rule of nature is that when a species exceeds the carrying capacity of its host environment, its food chains collapse and diseases emerge to devastate the population of the threatening organism. I believe we can come to balance with nature using mycelium to regulate the flow of nutrients. The age of mycological medicine is upon us. Now is the time to ensure the future of our planet and our species by partnering, or running, with mycelium."

—Paul Stamets, *Mycelium Running*

---

## MYCELIUM

Mycelium is the network of fungi and bacteria within the soil that connects tree roots, feeding the trees information and nutrients with the rich, decomposing materials of life.

Mycelium is nature's internet. We are still learning about this incredible underground network of knowledge, a web of life. According to fungi expert Paul Stamets, "mushrooms can help save the world." In his book *Mycelium Running*, Stamets writes, "Living in harmony with our natural environment is the key to health as individuals and as a species. We are a reflection of the environment that has given us birth."[78] If the macro-universe is polluted with toxins and chemicals, so is the micro-universe. Macro- and micro-universes are a mirror.

---

78 Stamets, Paul. Mycelium Running: How Mushrooms Can Help Save the World. Ten Speed Press - 2005.

Fungi and bacteria make up the majority of our lives. Our bodies are composed of about ten trillion cells, and only half of those are human cells. The other cells comprise our **microbiome**—a vast and complex ecosystem of bacteria, viruses, and fungi that live in or on our bodies.

"Think of your gut as an inner garden; just as with any garden—when you let the weeds take over, you get into trouble."

—Mark Hyman, MD[79]

---

## BACTERIA & FUNGI

Without microscopic bacteria and fungi, there would be no life. **Bacteria** were some of the first life-forms to surface on Earth,[80] and they exist in each breath we take and every bite we eat. Bacteria are everywhere.

Fungi are defined as any of a group of spore-producing organisms feeding on organic matter, including molds, yeast, mushrooms, and toadstools.

---

In our culture, we have become afraid of bacteria, over-sanitizing our hands and bodies, wiping or scrubbing

---

79 Mark Hyman, MD. Facebook Post, September 6, 2020. https://www.facebook.com/drmarkhyman/photos/a.163412217022869/3662867470410642/?type=3.

80 Sucher, Nikolaus. Laboratory Manual For Sci103 Biology I At Roxbury Community College. https://myrcc.rcc.mass.edu/ICS/103_lab_manual/archaea-and-bacteria.html.

away all the good bacteria that are here to protect us. Illness and sickness occur when our inner universe, our microbiome, has lost its balance. We are consumed by cleanliness—antibacterial *everything*, antibiotics in our food and medicine—and it is arguably making us sick.

Live, unpasteurized, fermented food is one of my favorite ways to bring back life, culture, and vibrancy to our communities. Maintaining a healthy culture of the right microorganisms and good bacteria is fundamental to vibrant health for us as individuals and for the planet. I enjoy feeding my body good bacteria to keep my immunity high by crafting kombucha, ginger beer, and sauerkraut each week (recipes in the Guided Inquiry at the end of this chapter).

"Bottom line: Fermentation makes food more nutritious and supports a healthy immune system."
—Love Probiotics[81]

Similar to the good bacteria in fermentation, fungi are the friends that decompose one kind of organic matter so that they can be reborn into another form.

---

81 Fermentation. Love Probiotics. http://www.loveprobiotics.org/.

## MYCELIUM PATH

"What once died turned into a mushroom.

To collect mushrooms in nature, we have to start by knowing them one by one. We need to know where a mushroom grows, how it looks in the sun and in the shade, what it smells like, how it looks from above and below, who its lookalikes are (the impostors), when it is harvested, how it is prepared, and on what moon.

Finding a mushroom is like meeting an old friend; we establish a relationship. Mushrooms help us, teach us, and guide us; and we recognize, protect, and care for them. Mutualistic symbiosis at its finest.

When you first leave your house, where are you going to go? Going to the forest, feeling the earth, and vibrating with nature might be the first things you would do. Luckily, I am in the jungle, with other challenges, living in a community.

My elders did not teach me about mushrooms. Many of them did not know them and were afraid of the unknown.

My interest in meeting them is uncontrollable. I want to go out into the edible forest and recognize my friends. Greet them and thank them for the meeting. Pick mushrooms and take them home to share."

–Lala Palmieri, Herbalist, Permaculture Teacher, Medicine Maker at @weaving.remedies and Ecology Academy @ecologyacademy[82]

---

82 www.ecologyacademy.com.

Fungi are a major part of every living organism, including the earth below our feet—the soil.

> "Soil is the great connector of lives, the source and destination of all. It is the healer and resurrector by which disease passes into health, age into youth, death into life. Without proper care for it we can have no community, because without proper care for it we can have no life."
>
> —Wendell Berry

Scientists have discovered that soil is one of the greatest solutions to our personal and planetary health concerns. When we consider that all our food and nutrients come from the soil, we see how it is all connected. We are all one living organism.

> "Let the beauty we love be what we do. There are hundreds of ways to kneel and kiss the ground."
>
> —Rumi

---

## WHY SOIL?

As part of my training on regenerative practices, I took a course on Soil Advocacy from Kiss the Ground.[83] I learned that soil is:

◎ The essential foundation and matrix for all life on land.

---

83  Soil Advocacy Training. Kiss the Ground. https://kisstheground.com/.

- ◎ The source of 95 percent of food that is produced.

- ◎ The base of all on-land diversity.

- ◎ The reason we have clean water sources.

- ◎ The most biodiverse ecosystem on the planet.

- ◎ A larger carbon pool than the atmosphere and biosphere combined.

- ◎ The most scalable solution and best carbon sink, with many additional benefits.

---

Building healthy soil through biodiversity, fungi, bacteria, and mycelium brings more prosperity to our farmers, our communities, and ultimately our planet. Just like fungi—which are everywhere and working all the time to decompose all matter—life, death, and rebirth are part of the cycle of existence.

∞

### 3/20/2019 Puerto Viejo, Costa Rica

*Opening like a flower each cycle,*
*In the mud,*
*Only to bloom as a*
*Lotus.*
*Or an avocado.*
*As we live, we share the gifts of life.*
*Seeing the beauty in the simple things.*
*The seeds. Coconuts. Flowers.*

*Feeling the ground.*
*Rooting down. Mixing soils. Cultures.*
*We must regenerate all relations.*
*Nurture the garden.*
*Connect in all ways.*
*Through each wave of life.*

∞

## CONCLUSION: DEATH, BACTERIA, & FUNGI

As I accepted my mother's death, I was compelled to live a fuller life than before, cherishing each day as if it could be my last. I think that when we accept the natural cycles of life, we start to see the interdependence of everything more clearly. We see and appreciate the bacteria that help us fight disease, the mycelium that runs beneath us, and the soils that nourish us. They are all part of the cycle of nature—of life itself.

May we accept that we are evolving; may we easefully shed our old selves to rebirth and blossom into radiant beings.

We have the ability to choose the path we walk and the life we live. Life goes by quickly, and we can choose to make it the kind of life we want to live. We can actively make each day great by practicing our passions and enjoying the dance of life. No matter what, we will all die in the end, returning to the soils. That is the natural cycle of life.

*The question is, when you return to the earth, will you leave the world better than you found it?*

"Walk as if you are kissing the Earth with your feet."
—Thich Nhat Hanh

"The meaning of life is just to be alive. It is so plain and so obvious and so simple, and yet, everyone rushes around in a great panic as if it were necessary to achieve something beyond themselves."

—Alan Watts

## LIVE UNTIL YOU DIE

"Is life dominated by chance?
Some changes are as subtle as the morning mist,
while others are giant beasts with the inevitable destiny to touch our paths.
Instead of resisting, what if we became receptive?

The essence of our human existence is simply to continue living, to thrive.
Perhaps the main obstacle that prevents us from understanding death
is that our unconscious is unable to accept that our existence must end.
Let's be willing to listen to our inner voice,
which tells us with certainty when to step into the unknown.

To lead a good life and thus die a good death,
we must make our decisions with unconditional love,
asking ourselves, "What service am I going to render with
this?"
Do what feels right, not what is expected of you.

Instead of being afraid, let's know ourselves.
All the hardships that we suffer in life, all the tribulations
and nightmares,
are opportunities to grow.
We cannot heal the world without first healing ourselves.
Each person chooses whether to emerge from difficulty
crushed or perfected.

Our today depends on our yesterday, and our tomorrow
depends on our today.
Have you loved yourself today?
Have you admired and thanked the flowers, appreciated
the birds, and contemplated the mountains, invaded by a
feeling of awe, reverence, and respect?

We all come from the same source and return to that same
source.
This is the ultimate lesson.
We must all learn to love and be loved unconditionally.

We must live until we die.

Let us live fully.

At the end of our days, we will bless our life, because we
have done what we came here to do.
Death is only a transition from this life to another existence
in which there is no more pain and anguish.
The only thing that lives forever is love."

–Diana Chaves,[84] Costa Rican Entrepreneur, Jungle
Project Co-founder and Community Developer

---

84 https://www.linkedin.com/in/diana-chaves-82b39b1a6/.

## Guided Inquiry

### Death and Composting

Compost is created from decomposed organic material, grass clippings, leaves, and kitchen waste. Composting is a way to connect with the natural cycles of life, death, and regeneration. It provides essential nutrients for plant growth and fertilizer for your garden and crops. Utilizing compost improves soil structure, adding back nutrients so that your soil can easily hold the correct amounts of moisture, nutrients, and air.

Compost closes the loop of your food cycle:
- Grow food
- Prepare food
- Produce scraps
- Compost
- Decompose food waste
- Use fertilizer in your garden
- Consume food

This beautiful food cycle is explained in more detail in Kiss the Ground's "Soil Story."[85] In addition, you can find our "How to Compost" videos directly from our garden on our website.

---

85 www.RegenerateYourReality.com and https://kisstheground.com/soil_story_curriculum_free_download/.

In short, here's how you can make your own compost right at home:

1. Choose your type of backyard compost bin or pile. We use a large metal barrel.

2. Put a bucket with a nice lid in your kitchen and label it as compost.

3. When you have filled your first compost bucket with food scraps and organic materials, bring it to your compost location, pour your organic scraps into the compost, and cover with a layer of dry leaves, soil, or wood chips.

4. Every few weeks, turn your compost with a shovel.

5. After your compost looks more like healthy soil than food waste, use it in your home garden or community garden to nourish and fertilize new life. The compost is ready to be harvested when the finished product is a rich dark brown color, smells like earth, and crumbles in your hand. (In the tropics, this could take about three months. In colder climates, it may be six to twelve months.)

### Fermentation

Fermentation describes the transformative action of microorganisms. I feel that it is so relevant to talk about in this chapter because fermented food undergoes a process of decomposition by live bacteria, which strengthens our immune systems. Fermentation has been around since the beginning of human history. We have the Greek god of wine, Dionysus, the blood of Jesus Christ in consecrated wine, and the food of the gods, cacao, fermented into chocolate. Humans have evolved with our fermentation of beverages and food.

Even though most of our favorite foods have traditionally always been fermented (beer, wine, chocolate, tea, cheese, bread, etc.), many commercially available fermented foods are pasteurized, which means they are heated to the point that all microorganisms die. This process renders the food "lifeless." Live, fermented food helps us build back good bacteria in our gut, which then fight off illness and keep us thriving. Each week, I like to brew kombucha and non-alcoholic ginger beer, and I regularly make fruit vinegar and sauerkraut. This is a key part of my ongoing health rituals to regenerate my reality.

I invite you to start making your own probiotics or fermented foods at home. You can start with fruit scrap vinegar and work your way up from there to more complex fermentations. Start experimenting with your own medicines! Head to our website for more recipes provided by Love Probiotics,[86] inspired by *Wild Fermentation* by Sandor Katz.[87]

---

86 "Love Probiotics," (Love Probiotics, 2016), http://www.loveprobiotics.org/.
87 Sandor Ellix Katz, *Wild Fermentation: A Do-It-Yourself Guide to Cultural Manipulation* (Microcosm Publishing, 2017).

## FRUIT SCRAP VINEGAR
### Ingredients:

- ¼ cup (60 mL) raw, organic sugar
- Fruit scraps (apple, pineapple, or banana peels, grapes, berries, etc.)
- Water

### Process:

1. **In a jar or bowl, dissolve the sugar in one quart (1 L) of water.** Coarsely chop the fruit peels and add to the sugar water.

2. **Cover the jar or bowl with cheesecloth** to keep flies out, and leave to ferment at room temperature.

3. When you notice the liquid darkening (after about one week), strain out the peels and discard.

4. **Ferment the liquid for three to four weeks more,** stirring or agitating periodically. Then your fruit scrap vinegar will be ready to use!

## Wisdom Questions

♥ Are you afraid of death? What does that fear feel like?

♥ How do you experience the cycles of life in big or small ways?

♥ In what ways have you "died" in order to be born again?

♥ What cultures and bacteria can you cultivate in your home or body?

# CONCLUSION:
# SHORT WRITINGS, PRAYERS, & POEMS

**Affirmation: I am an artist of each moment. I am blessed to be alive. I create my own reality with each thought, word, and action.**

*"Trees we plant today are forests we enjoy tomorrow.*

The 7 Secrets of Happiness

1. Think positively.

2. Do work you love.

3. Avoid anger.

4. Give generously.

5. Be grateful.

6. Overcome negativity.

7. Develop thick skin."

—Matshona Dhliwayo

∞

When I started to prepare to write this book, I reread seven years' worth of journals. I initially thought that

*Regenerate Your Reality* would be more of a memoir of journal entries than a guidebook, but then all the lessons I recorded in my journals coalesced into the teachings I continue to need—and wish to share, too.

This process of remembering and reliving my experiences has been deeply healing for me. It has empowered me to invest in my book-writing dream with lots of energy and love. I never thought I could write or be an author, but now I have overcome this self-limiting belief. Creating this book has filled me with so much joy!

We are all artists with the capacity to create in so many different forms. All we need is the right environment and inspiration to fuel us. Today more than ever, we need to help restore the harmony of the earth through our unique offerings and love for living. We are all dancing together in this symphony of life, playing our parts beautifully. Every instrument or being is an important part of the whole.

We all matter. My wish is that we may celebrate our differences and share our gifts.

∞

May this book spark change, action, and awareness. I believe that we have the power to continually regenerate ourselves and this earth. May we continue to shed old programming, ways of being, and belief systems that do not support us in love. May we live our regeneration in all ways.

**I'd like to conclude by reviewing some of the key lessons from this journey:**

&#9758; In Chapter 1, we learned to live our dreams every day, ground our passions in action, and remember that we are holistic beings.

**Affirmation: I take action on my dreams every day.**

&#9758; In Chapter 2, we asked, "What is my fire? What is my passion path?" We discovered permaculture, regeneration in all its dimensions, and the importance of planting trees and developing community projects. We also learned about diversity in crops and regenerative agriculture.

**Affirmation: I make my dream my reality through my actions and passions. I follow the call of my heart and intuition.**

&#9758; In Chapter 3, we looked at different pathways to becoming financially free, living more simply, consuming consciously, investing in ourselves and our passions, and living diversity in every way. We saw how our time is our most valuable asset. We are meant to thrive. Abundance is our birthright.

**Affirmation: I draw my personal abundance from an infinite source.**

⊚ In Chapter 4, we discovered purification methods to regenerate the body and mind. We navigated paths to regeneration through meditation, movement, silence, and organic foods. We considered that when we restore our love for ourselves and our lives, we can then fully show up in service to others and to the earth.

**Affirmation: I am whole. I am in vibrant health. With each breath comes a new opportunity. I choose to make today a great day.**

⊚ In Chapter 5, we explored the love that exists within us and around us all the time. We considered that love is a state of being we can feel often, if we choose. We also discovered the connection between self-love and seeds as the foundations of life and saw how seeds must be protected and planted in our gardens, just like love.

**Affirmation: I am love. Love is within me. Love surrounds me.**

⊚ In Chapter 6, we learned all about our plant allies and plant medicines. We focused on using food as our medicine through soups, sauces, ferments, and more, and we explored healing with herbalism, as well as our love for cacao and our potential for expansion and growth with hallucinogens such as psilocybin and DMT.

**Affirmation: Plants are my allies. Plants are my medicine. Plants are a Queendom; they connect me to the universe.**

In Chapter 7, we talked about death and rebirth. Why do we fear death so much? We considered that death is life and life is death. It is all one and the same, a cycle. We looked at the interconnected relationship between death, fungi, mushrooms, and soil, and we learned about soil as a regenerative solution to protect the health of our planet and all beings.

**Affirmation: I embrace death, rebirth, and the cycles of life. I know I am made of many bacteria and fungi. I am a living, live organism. I am vibrantly alive.**

∞

## Mantra for Regeneration

*Action speaks.*

*Words must be impeccable.*

*Do the best you can.*

*Don't take anything personally.*

*F.L.Y. (First. Love. Yourself.)*

*Serve others how you want to be treated.*

*Receive and give.*

*Listen to intuition.*

*Empower farmers.*

*Check in with your heart.*

*Follow your passions.*

*Protect this earth.*

*Stand as a steward of the lands.*

∞

**These lessons are just the first step. Regeneration is all about action. Here are a few of my favorite action steps to get you started:**

- ◎ Plant a garden—at home, at your neighborhood school, in any free spaces, or in pots, indoors or outdoors.

- ◎ Buy local and organic as much as possible.

- ◎ Reestablish your connection to the earth and your food. Start a compost! Get to know your farmers. Forage in the forest.

- ◎ Loving yourself means loving this planet. Get outside and spend time in the woods, mountains, or any other place in nature.

- ◎ Reducing your carbon footprint begins with a single step: awareness. What is your carbon footprint? What steps can you take to be carbon-neutral? Planting trees or donating to support tree planting is a great place to start.[88]

- ◎ Start activating your dreams by living them into reality.

- ◎ Give back to your local community with time, resources, or partnerships.

∞

To conclude this final chapter, I would like to share a few additional poems and prayers from my journals that resonate hope, love, and awareness.

88 Jungle Project (Jungle Project, 2020), https://jungleproject.com.

I hope you feel as inspired as I do to continue down this path of regeneration. It is not always the easiest, and it requires radical transparency, constant communication with your intuition and heart, and an ongoing investigation of your and the earth's needs. We are forces of nature, and we can work together to leave our home better than we found it.

# PRAYERS & POEMS

### Fairy Garden

*Happiness is:*
*feeling connected to nature,*
*living in a secret garden,*
*where I play in the present moment.*
*Living in love.*

*We choose to live in heaven or hell.*
*In our mind.*
*In our surroundings.*
*We attract what we are.*

*When we experience darkness and negativity,*
*may we sit and observe it.*
*Where it roots,*
*may we transmute it into love.*
*May we live in harmony with nature,*
*breaking patterns that run deep.*

*May we work together to regenerate*
*our minds.*

*Cultivating peace.*

*Trusting.*

*Transforming*

*our lawns, cow pastures, monoculture crops*

*with trees that feed.*

*Freeing*

*oceans and rivers of plastics.*

*As we feel the earth,*

*may we reforest.*

*May the oceans thrive.*

*May we keep hope.*

∞

## Let's Rewild

*The energy we put out is either polluting or healing.*
*Which do we choose?*
*Do we want to focus on the solution or the problem?*

*Our focus is on the solution.*

*Helping protect this earth, connecting to the rhythms and*
*patterns that repeat in everything.*

*We are 70 percent water,*
*Trees are too.*
*Our veins are the veins of rivers,*
*flowing across the earth, our flesh, ourselves.*

*When we tune into this energy of being one,*
*of being from this earth,*
*with no borders or walls or fences,*
*this is when true community begins.*

*When we love,*
*we heal ourselves,*
*and we become leaders within the community*
*through example and service.*

*Collective consciousness is a field of energy we can all tap into.*

*We are all divine beings, children from the same Mother.*

*Our connection with the animals and plants and earth can be the same as our connection with our loved ones:*

*Protecting them as we would want to be treated ourselves.*

*Let's rewild ourselves:*

*To live our complete truth.*
*To live within the wild.*
*To dance in trance doing acrobatics.*

*To fly with our scarves.*
*To walk barefoot.*

*To talk and sing to blue morpho butterflies:*
*"Hola bonita hermosa, vuela! Vuela conmigo."*

*To explore tidal pools that are fairy ponds,*
*home to thousands of fish and many new species we have not yet discovered.*

*To listen to monkeys and call them in.*

*To talk to parrots and green macaws.*

*Turning our fear into love. Living love. Being love.*
*Treating everyone with as much love as we give ourselves.*

∞

### Solstice Prayer

*Dear God,*
*I pray for trust,*
*holding boundaries,*
*having courage,*
*finding my center,*
*knowing the tools are there.*

*I pray to ground down, remembering and trusting the path,*
*following my heart,*
*knowing my value,*
*allowing my mind to be present.*

*I pray that all connections align,*
*that heart-centered people unite all the colors of the rainbow,*
*all being,*
*co-thriving—*
*the collective vision turns into action.*

*I pray for wholeness of self and wholeness of all*
*our bodies and temples.*
*We care for the environment and the environmentalist.*

*Sun shines through us—*
*let each star rise.*

∞

## Create Reality

*Life. I make it.*
*We create it.*
*Knowing what I need,*
*I must take it*
*to fill me*
*with light.*
*Nature is calling.*

*The waves invite me in.*
*Butterflies lead me.*
*The jungle paves the path.*

*We are children,*
*playing*
*like puppies.*

*All I can do is enjoy this.*
*It could be all we have.*
*Four puppies we are,*
*holding energy and oozing with joy.*
*The pureness is contagious.*
*Smiling. Sharing. Laughing.*

*Star Child, bright-eyed.*
*There is always abundance.*
*I am open to receive:*
*Friends. Blessings.*

*That's the path*
*I trust.*

*The people in the present are my angels.*
*All I need to do is look into their eyes.*

*I am so grateful for the love from all aspects of life.*
*Thankful for the sun and the rains.*
*I feel the waves,*
*float in them,*
*mermaid time with all the beings,*
*splashing and playing,*
*respecting the water,*
*puppies swimming,*
*children playing.*

*Life is good.*
*What a beautiful mess.*
*I am held. We are okay.*
*"Todo es posible."*

*Yes, each day is new.*

*I write this to myself as a positive affirmation,*
*turning my words to reality.*
*Turning fear, death, and sorrow into transformation.*

*Cycles. Love. Joy.*
*I pray that I may continue to feed my soul.*

∞

## Joy Ride of Life

*When we step back and let happiness lead the way, we
enter a state of joy.
We leave a positive imprint on every being in the world.
Each action has an equal reaction.*

*I went on a journey to seek my happiness, measuring
everything on a scale of
Yes, this makes me excited or
No, I need to change something.*

*I create my own reality with
enthusiasm for each moment,
doing what I feel called to do,
called to learn, to try, to make, and to experiment—
Why not?*

*We are all teaching and learning new ways.
Who says what is right?
There are so many ways.*

*By tuning like a guitar and singing from the heart,
this frequency, no matter what language is spoken, is an
energy exchange—
there is no barrier.*

*We make walls by not being
present,
not feeling, knowing, or seeing.*

*When we are open to receive, we will receive
more than we ever imagined:
Wealth in the form of care, help, food, rides,
and giving all that we can, always.*

*Hearts converse in the language of love.*

∞

## Intentions

1. ***Love.*** *I allow each thought, action, and word to come from my heart.*

2. ***Regenerate.*** *I regenerate myself each day, restoring the earth and my communities.*

3. ***Trust.*** *I embrace the unknown as the greatest magical mystery, knowing that all is divine. I make choices that align with my deepest desires and my heart's path.*

4. ***Boundaries.*** *I am able to trust my intuition and say "no" when necessary.*

5. ***Unity.*** *I am never alone. We are always in this together.*

6. ***Family.*** *Relationships grow through radical communication.*

∞

## Rainbow Bridge

*We choose freedom.*
*The only way out of crisis is*
*growing our way out of it—*
*literally.*

*We support local, organic practices*
*and cultivate our own garden,*
*securing fresh water sources,*
*becoming sovereign.*

*We must act collectively,*
*shift habits.*
*Grow and expand together.*

*May all beings be free and happy,*
*in harmony with nature.*

*We choose love—*
*A bridge between all colors and worlds.*

∞

## Prayer for the New Year

*Dear Mama Earth,*

*We wake up today feeling a shift, excitement for this new decade, and hope for harmony.*
*We feel our awakening. Our unity. The collective rise of so many.*

*I pray for radical self-love for each heart.*
*I pray that we may accept ourselves as part of the earth, air, water, and fire.*

*I pray that each being may become whole,*
*that each individual may discover the power of choice and create collective change.*

*A ripple of evolution is converting our systems to circular economies, connecting us to nature,*
*to each bite of food. To each other.*
*I pray people, governments, and corporations come together with the shared purpose to regenerate our home planet.*

*I pray that we may remember how to live simply.*
*I pray that we plant abundant food forests to feed future generations.*

*I pray that we keep growing together,*
*keep dancing and singing,*
*to harmonize all.*

*We pray for balance, wholeness, freedom, and harmony of*
*all beings.*

∞

## Medicine Song
*Adapted from Devananda Lal,*[89] *"Gathering the flowers"*

*Gathering the faeries,*
*faeries of the forest*

*Forest full of medicine*
*to help us with our healing*

*Healing of our bodies*
*Body, mind, and spirit*

*Spirit of the sisterhood come and*
*embrace all our hearts*

*Heart is feeling open*
*opening empowered*

*Empowering the faeries*
*to come together*
*Gather.*

∞

---

89 Devananda Lal, "Gathering the flowers." https://singingalive.org/2015/12/03/gathering-the-flowers/.

"Just like moons and like suns,

With the certainty of tides,

Just like hopes springing high,

Still I'll rise."

—*Maya Angelou*

∞

*Let's leave this earthship better than we found it!*

# ACKNOWLEDGMENTS

Thank you, God, for this existence.

Thank you, Mother Earth.

Gratitude for my mother, Kay, and father, Edward, for making me from love.

Thanks to my brother and best friend, Brett.

Thank you to my loving partner, Alan, who has co-created our dreams of sovereignty into reality.

Gratitude to my editor, Toby, who helped mentor me and edit this book.

Thank you to all the cosmic family and angels who enter my life, making it sweeter.

Gratitude for all the sisters and special contributors who have held me through all the waves of life.

And for the ocean waters for their magnificent and healing energies.

Thank you to the jungle and all the biodiversity.

Gratitude for the fruitful land that surrounds us.

Gratitude for allowing my heart to lead.

Thank you to all the environmentalists taking action to love this earth.

Thank you, Costa Rica, the heart center of the Americas.

# APPENDIX

## SUGGESTED READING LIST

### *Plant:*

Katz, Sandor Ellix. *Wild Fermentation: A Do-It-Yourself Guide to Cultural Manipulation.* Microcosm Publishing, 2017.

Rodale, Maria. *Organic Manifesto: How Organic Farming Can Heal Our Planet, Feed the World, and Keep Us Safe.* New York: Rodale, 2011.

Tompkins, Peter, and Christopher Bird. *The Secret Life of Plants.* New York: Harper & Row, 1973.

Elevitch, Craig R, and Diane Ragone. "Breadfruit Agroforestry Guide: Planning and Implementation of Regenerative Organic Methods." www.ntbg.org/breadfruit. Breadfruit Institute of the National Tropical Botanical Garden, Kalaheo, Hawaii and Permanent Agriculture Resources, Holualoa, Hawaii, 2018. https://ntbg.org/wp-content/uploads/2020/02/breadfruit_agroforestry_guide_web_edition.pdf.

Schultes, Richard Evans, and Albert Hofmann. *Plants of the Gods.* McGraw Hill, 1979.

Buettner, Dan, and David McLain. *The Blue Zones Kitchen: 100 Recipes to Live to 100*. Washington, D.C.: National Geographic, 2019.

Mollison, Bill, and Andrew Jeeves. *Permaculture: A Designers' Manual*. Sisters Creek, Tasmania: Tagari Publications, 2014.

***Grow:***
Gilbert, Elizabeth. *Big Magic*. New York, NY: Penguin Publishing Group, 2016.

Murphy, Ryan, and Elizabeth Gilbert. *Eat Pray Love*. New York, NY: Riverhead Books, 2011.

Gladwell, Malcolm. *The Tipping Point: How Little Things Can Make a Big Difference*. Little, Brown and Company, 2019.

Angelou, Maya, and Joanne M. Braxton. *Maya Angelou's I Know Why the Caged Bird Sings: A Casebook*. New York, NY: Oxford Univ. Press, 1999.

Wohlleben, Peter. *The Hidden Life of Trees*. Vancouver: David Suzuki Institute, Greystone Books, 2018.

Israel, Toby. *Vagabondess: A Guide to Solo Female Travel*. Toby Israel, LLC, 2020.

Pollan, Michael. *The Omnivore's Dilemma: A Natural History of Four Meals*. New York, NY: Penguin Press, 2016.

Pollan, Michael. *How to Change Your Mind: The New Science of Psychedelics*. London: Penguin Books, 2019.

### Expand:

Redfield, James. *The Celestine Prophecy: An Adventure*. New York, NY: Grand Central Publishing, 2018.

Ruiz, Don Miguel. *The Mastery of Love: A Practical Guide to the Art of Relationship*. San Rafael, CA: Amber-Allen Publishing, 1999.

Ruiz, Miguel. *The Four Agreements: A Practical Guide to Personal Freedom*. San Rafael, CA: Amber-Allen Publishing, 2017.

Tolle, Eckhart. *The Power of Now: A Guide to Spiritual Enlightenment*. Sydney, NSW: Hachette Australia, 2018.

Campbell, Rebecca. *Rise Sister Rise: A Guide to Unleashing the Wise, Wild Woman Within*. Carlsbad, CA: Hay House, 2016.

Bertrand, Azra. *Womb Awakening: Initiatory Wisdom from the Creatrix of All Life*. Rochester, VT: Bear & Company, 2017.

Éstes Clarissa Pinkola. *Women Who Run with Wolves: Myths and Stories of the Wild Women Archetype.* New York, NY: Ballantine Books, 1995.

Bertrand, Azra. *Womb Awakening: Initiatory Wisdom from the Creatrix of All Life.* Rochester, Vermont: Bear & Company, 2017.

Ashé Danielle, and Jane Astara Ashley. *Ancient-Future Unity: Reclaim Your Roots, Liberate Your Lineage, Live a Legacy of Love.* Old Saybrook, CT: Flower of Life Press, 2021.

## RECOMMENDED DOCUMENTARIES & VIDEOS

- Betz, Jon and Taggart Siegel, dirs. *SEED: The Untold Story*. Independent Lens, 2016.

- Sustainable Human, "How Wolves Change Rivers." *YouTube* video, 4:17. November 15, 2017. https://www.youtube.com/watch?v=ysa5OBhXz-Q&t=13s.

- TED, "How to green the world's deserts and reverse climate change | Allan Savory." *YouTube* video, 22:19. March 4, 2013. https://www.youtube.com/watch?v=vpTHi7O66pI&t=2s.

- TEDx Talks, "Regenerative Culture | Finian Makepeace | TEDxSantaCruz." *YouTube* video, 14:51. June 11, 2020. https://www.youtube.com/watch?v=81bYrqhoAyo.

- TEDx Talks, "Salvation Is In Soil | Florence Reed | TEDxDirigo." *YouTube* video, 13:16. December 15, 2017. https://www.youtube.com/watch?v=UYVxo29x7vM.

- Morgan, Faith, dir. *The Power of Community: How Cuba Survived Peak Oil*. The Community Solution, 2006.

- Caracol Producciones, "Sipakapa No Se Vende (Subtítulos Inglés)." *YouTube* video, 56:17. April 4, 2014. https://youtu.be/F36SqLpqQmQ.

- Tickell, Rebecca, dir. *Kiss the Ground.* Big Picture Ranch, 2020. https://www.netflix.com/title/81321999.

- Fulkerson, Lee, dir. *Forks over Knives.* Monica Beach Media, 2011.

- *Down to Earth with Zac Efron.* Netflix Originals, 2020. https://www.netflix.com/title/80230601.

- Scholey, Keith, Hughes, Johnathan, and Alastair Fothergill, dirs. *David Attenborough: A Life on Our Planet.* Netflix Originals, 2020. https://www.netflix.com/title/80216393.

- Tabrizi, Ali, dir. *Seaspiracy.* Netflix Originals, 2021. https://www.netflix.com/title/81014008.

- Anderson, Kipp and Keegan Kuhn, dirs. *Cowspiracy: The Sustainability Secret.* Appian Way Productions, 2014. https://www.netflix.com/title/80033772.

- Lanfear, Sophie, dir. *Our Planet.* Netflix Originals, 2019. https://www.netflix.com/title/80049832.

- D'Avella, Matt, dir. *Minimalism: A Documentary About The Important Things.* Netflix Originals, 2016. https://www.netflix.com/title/80114460.

- Anderson, Kipp and Keegan Kuhn, dirs. *What the Health.* Netflix Originals, 2017. https://www.netflix.com/title/80174177.

- Schultz, Mitch, dir. *DMT: The Spirit Molecule*. 2010.

- Stevens, Fisher, dir. *Before the Flood*. National Geographic, 2016.

- Chester, John, dir. *The Biggest Little Farm*. Neon, 2018.

- Herring, Rob and Ryan Wirick, dirs. *The Need to Grow*. 2018.

## ECOLOGICAL CENTERS TO VISIT

- Our Farm at Regenerate Your Reality—Fairy Farm, Costa Rica https://www.regenerateyourreality.com/.

- Finca La Isla Permaculture Farm, Costa Rica https://www.costaricaorganicsfarm.com/.

- Madre Tierra, Costa Rica https://fincatierra.com/.

- Finca Madre, Paul Zink, Costa Rica https://www.airbnb.com/experiences/124239.

- Jungle Project, Various Communities, Costa Rica https://jungleproject.com/.

- Rancho Mastatal, Costa Rica https://ranchomastatal.com/.

- Rancho Margot, Costa Rica https://www.ranchomargot.com/.

- Finca Luna Nueva, Costa Rica https://fincalunanuevalodge.com/.

- Essence Arenal, Costa Rica http://essencearenal.com/.

- Las Cañadas, Mexico https://bosquedeniebla.com.mx/.

- Mystical Yoga Farm, Guatemala https://mysticalyogafarm.com/.

- Earth University Organic Farming, Costa Rica https://www.earth.ac.cr/en/.

- Punta Mona, Costa Rica https://www.puntam-ona.org/.

## ABOUT REGENERATE YOUR REALITY

I am the founder of this project—a live seed bank and a model of sovereignty. Regenerate Your Reality is a community project that started in our own backyard with spreading seeds, preserving biodiversity, planting trees, teaching interactive holistic earth workshops, consulting agroforestry projects, and guiding regenerative agriculture tours. Regenerate Your Reality is transforming from our garden and community project into a book and hub for regenerative educational resources online and on the ground, touring with us!

The RegenerateYourReality.com website has many videos, links, guides, and information to support your path of regeneration. Some of the proceeds from this book go back to planting trees and gardens and providing resources to women and children in need. World hunger, malnutrition, and global warming are the biggest crises of our lifetime. We have the ability to be the generation that acts to create solutions. To create a better tomorrow.

Plant. Grow. Expand.

***The Gift that Keeps on Giving! Plant Trees.***

*A portion of the proceeds from this book will benefit the Trees, Training, Trade Program by Jungle Project in partnership with the Kiss the Ground nonprofit organization, whose combined missions are to preserve the quality of our soils and water through regenerative farming and agroforestry. We believe Regenerative Agriculture can reverse climate change, while providing a solution for malnutrition and world hunger.*

*Learn more at*
*https://www.regenerateyourreality.com/takeaction.*

# ABOUT THE AUTHOR

Jean Pullen has felt called to environmentalism since a young age. In 2017, she moved to Costa Rica to follow her passion for regenerating nature through permaculture, agroforestry, and community.

Jean is the founder of Regenerate Your Reality, a resource for those who seek regeneration in their lives and in the world. She is a partner of Jungle Project and a Soil Advocate at Kiss the Ground. In addition, she enjoys sharing her passions through holistic workshops and regenerative agriculture tours.

Jean lives with her partner, Alan, and their dog, Pata Blanca, on their beautiful jungle farm in Costa Rica. She enjoys gardening, cooking, singing, and making art. Her ultimate dream is to educate others on how they can bolster biodiversity and combat climate change through regenerative action.

Learn more at www.regenerateyourreality.com